THE GUARDIANS

FIVE TRUE STORIES OF COAST GUARD
HEROES AND THEIR RESCUES IN NEW
ORLEANS FOLLOWING HURRICANE KATRINA

DARREL CREACY AND CARLITO VICENCIO

The Real Guardians

Darrel Creacy and Carlito Vicencio

Dude Productions, Inc.
3302 Farmington Street
Houston, TX 77080
866-799-DUDE (3833)

Find us on the World Wide Web at: www.therealguardians.com.

Visit our other sites at: www.dudecomputers.com and www.dudebooks.com.

To contact us, please send a note to carlito@dudebooks.com or darrel@dude-books.com. You can report errors to these emails as well.

Copyright © 2006 by Darrel Creacy and Carlito Vicencio
Cover Design: Martin Vives & Darrel Creacy
Interior Design and Layout: Martin Vives
Chief Editor: Beth Williams
Contributing Editors: Carlito S. Vicencio, Sherrie Vicencio, John Williams
Xaimara Vicencio-Roldan, and Michael Comess
Web Design: Veronika Joannides (www.teamdudeproductions.com)

Notice of Rights

Notice of Liability

ISBN 0978961900

Printed and bound in the United States of America

This book is dedicated
to the men and women of the United States Coast Guard.

Table of Contents

Acknowledgements

Special thanks to LT Sean O'Brien, LT Charles Guerrero, LT Jason Smith, AST3 Charles Medema and AST3 David McClure for sharing their stories with us and to their wives and family for supporting their noble career choice. You humble young men did your nation proud, keep up the good work!! We'd also like to extend a special thanks to the men and women of the U.S. Coast Guard who sacrifice so much and expect nothing in return for their hard work and dedication. This nation is forever in your debt.

To the great friends and family that supported this project, we say "thank you so much!" We've been extremely blessed to be surrounded by such supportive people in our lives. If it were not for the support of our friends and family who read a chapter here or a chapter there, this book would not have been able to go out on time.

Beth Williams thanks for going through practically every single word in this book for us!

We also want to express our sincere appreciation to CWO Adam Wine and his staff for the wonderful pictures that were shared with us to be included in this book.

And finally, last but not least, we'd like to say "great job and thanks" to Martin Vives who designed this kick ass cover and designed the layout for this entire manuscript. You are an awesome friend and talented graphic designer. This wouldn't have been possible without you. We'll definitely work with you in future projects. You rock!!

The Coast Guard Mutual Assistance Foundation

Proceeds from the royalties of this book will be donated to the Coast Guard Mutual Assistance (CGMA) Foundation. In one way or another every Coastie has benefited from this great organization that helps Coasties when they need help most. Whether receiving a loan to fix a broken down car or seeing a friend receive financial assistance to repair a leaky water heater, we've all seen CGMA aid a Coastie in need.

About the Authors

Darrel Creacy is a recently retired Coast Guard helicopter pilot who earned two United States Air Medals during his career, and was directly responsible for saving more than 50 lives. The heroic deeds and intense rescue stories from Hurricane Katrina brought back memories from his own heroic Air Medal rescues and inspired Darrel to co-author this book.

Carlito Vicencio is a former Coast Guard helicopter pilot who earned a United States Air Medal for heroic actions during Hurricane Katrina rescue efforts. As his Air Medal Citation reads, Carlito's "actions and aeronautical skill were instrumental in saving 122 lives." After sharing Hurricane Katrina stories with his good friend Darrel, he too was inspired to co-author this book.

To Our Dear Families

We would like to take a special opportunity to express our sincere gratitude to our wives, Cheri Creacy and Sherrie Vicencio. Thank you for your continued support as we pursue our personal goals and aspirations. We realize the sacrifices you make and the burden our second jobs as authors and businessmen place on our families. We appreciate your patience, love and support.

To our children we offer this advice for your futures,
"Find that one thing that inspires you to be extraordinary."

To Our Readers

Darrel and Carlito are honored to share these "sea stories of the future" with all of you. The heroic actions by Coast Guard aircrews during Hurricane Katrina cannot go forgotten or untold. We hope to capture just a little bit of what happened and with these significant events, have something to always remember this great Humanitarian Mission. Thanks for allowing us to share these accounts with you.

INTRODUCTION

In 1790, a fledgling nation in dire need of revenue and control over trade established an organization to protect the sovereign shores of America. Faced with building this new nation, Congress chartered the Revenue Cutter Service to enforce laws that would govern maritime activities. It was necessary to legitimize this uncontrolled trade and to generate revenue from the open peddling that was taking place. The Revenue Cutter Service in its early beginning consisted of 10 ships and was given the daunting task of enforcing the tariff collection that would fund the building of our great nation. In its charter, the United States Coast Guard (USCG), then the Revenue Cutter Service, found itself "The Real Guardians" of the nation.

As America continued to grow, so did the need to protect its citizens. In a maritime sense, this meant a more unified effort along the shores. Because of this reality, in 1915 Congress decided to merge two like-minded agencies, the Revenue Cutter Service and the Life Saving Service which was a loosely organized group entrusted with fast response to immediate peril along the shorelines. This simple, yet benevolent fusion spawned the multiple mission concept. Together these two agencies were stronger, with ships, boats and men possessing different talents. This act took the notion of protecting citizens from peril and broadened its reach to mariners at sea. This established the USCG we know today with its proud tradition of protecting all aspects of life at sea, whether it be cargo ships en-route to port with their valuable goods or a young child that gets swept away by the surf.

At that point, the USCG was then in charge of developing the means to execute those multiple missions. As the old saying goes "necessity is the mother of invention." Pioneers, LT Elmer Stone and LT Norman Hall envisioned a way to utilize the emerging technology of aircraft to get there faster, safer, and more effectively. After several failed attempts at incorporating air capabilities into the Search and Rescue business, the value was finally realized and, in 1926, the leaders of the USCG funded and built the first permanent Coast Guard Air Station in Cape May, NJ. From that day forth, if anyone at sea was in distress in or around the sovereign waters of the United States, they knew if the call went out to the USCG, that these Guardians would swoop in from above to render assistance.

Today's modern Coast Guard is a multi-faceted organization entrusted with Maritime Safety, Maritime Mobility, Maritime Security and Homeland Defense. They use ships, aircraft, people, computers and weapons to get the job done. Everyday, 24 hours a day 7 days a week, Coasties around the nation are standing watch waiting to take the call whether it be a terrorist threat, a broken buoy, an oil spill or a mariner in distress. These unsung heroes don't ask for much and fulfill their job with pride.

As valuable and honorable as all these missions are, there exists an elite group known as "Bravo Zero." These are the men and women of the Coast Guard who are the first responders, they truly are the life savers. They sleep next to an alarm waiting for the next Search and Rescue call. This elite group consists of the small boat stations waiting to launch and get underway and the air stations equipped with helicopters. Both are trained with the skills and provided the equipment to rise from a dead sleep and be underway or airborne in 30 minutes or less. Every Coastie knows however, that the helicopter crews usually get there first.

The day came, August 29, 2005, when all the training, hard work, and sacrifice were put to the ultimate test. Hurricane Katrina, a category-5 storm had been bearing down on the Gulf Coast for the past 3 days and had her

sights set on the Louisiana/Mississippi coast. In the final hours before landfall the nation knew that she would hit close to the border of the two states. The cities of New Orleans, Gulfport, Biloxi and many others along the coast were in the midst of mass evacuations with hundreds of thousands of people in the crosshairs of this devastating storm.

Along with all the other evacuees, the Coast Guard men and women stationed in Louisiana and Mississippi sent their families to evacuate, then they took their equipment to safe harbors. Our heroes flew their aircrafts to places like Houston to lay-in-wait for the storm to pass. As the eye of the storm passed the shoreline, plans had already been formulated to send these brave crews into the devastated areas to save the helpless individuals left behind. Our stories will focus on the heroic efforts of five truly brave Guardians that risked their lives to save others. You'll find their stories inspirational and compelling. Honor, respect and devotion to duty are concepts that most people don't understand, but these fine people live, breath and sleep these core values, so when the worst should happen there's somebody to call that will show up no matter what.

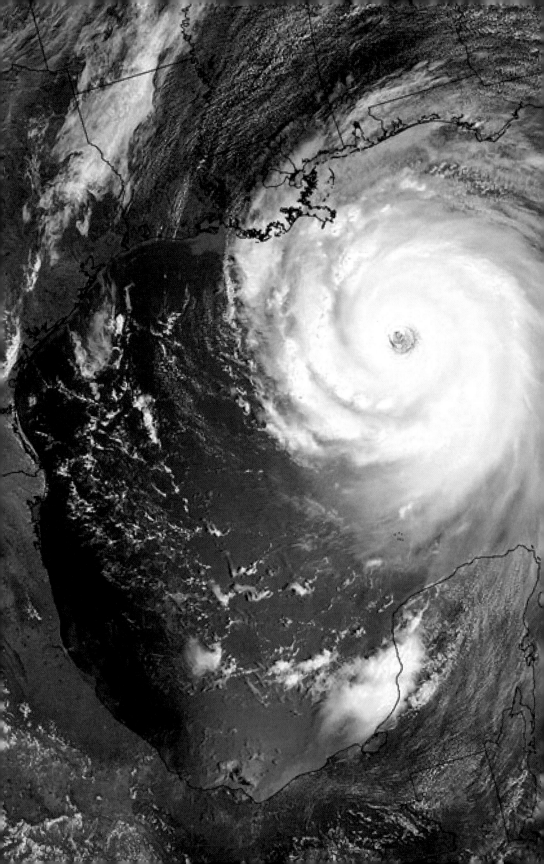

Category 5 Storm Develops

After teasing the nation as a Category 1 hurricane by hitting southern Florida and causing minimal damage, Katrina entered the Gulf of Mexico. The Gulf, with its warm waters and hot humid conditions, is ideal for tropical storm growth and acts as an incubator for storms to blossom into mega-hurricanes in a short time frame. These perfect conditions fed Katrina into maturity as a Category 5 hurricane, making Katrina the focus of national attention.

At sea, NOAA buoys were measuring waves at 40 to 50 feet, making the storm surge the most daunting part of Hurricane Katrina. Her winds were now registering sustained speeds in excess of 155 miles per hour, mandatory and voluntary evacuation plans were well underway in the target zone. From eastern Texas to the Alabama panhandle, people were mobilizing a retreat from the impending attack that was Katrina. Millions of people boarded-up their homes, fueled their cars, and gathered a few priceless possessions with the hopes of escaping Katrina's lethal punch.

As Katrina's inevitable rampage approached land, Coast Guard Air Station Houston's Commanding Officer, Captain Norman Schweizer, as did all Gulf Coast units prepared for the worst. Plans that had been developed from years of experience with storms similar to Katrina were finalized and executed. The scenarios that had been possibilities since she moved across Florida began to lessen and the probabilities began to rise, Katrina was going to hit Louisiana or Mississippi. The District 8 Commander, Rear Admiral Robert Duncan, knew that his coastline was about to become the subject of national focus and devastation on a global scale. With keen foresight, he authorized early evacuation of CG families knowing that their best chance for survival was to get out early. He also realized that removing the anxiety of their families' safety from his active duty personnel would allow the first responders to focus on the rescue efforts that lie ahead.

Coast Guard Air Stations nationwide were also finalizing their mobilization plans to launch their aircrews to help in anyway they could. When something as devastating as Katrina ravages one CG unit it ravages all of them. Commanding Officers of all Coast Guard Air Stations volunteered their pilots, aircrews, helicopters and airplanes days before Katrina made landfall. Coast Guard Air Stations nationwide had demanding and ambitious duty schedules in place that would allow them to meet their missions and support relief operations along the Gulf. The Atlantic Area Commander, VADM Vivien Crea led the way, running operations in the New Orleans Area along with her District staff. Already doing more with less, supporting a national relief effort put a great burden on all CG personnel and families, but as their motto goes, the CG was "Semper Paratus". Semper Paratus means "Always Ready", and these CG heroes did not only possess the skill, talent and dedication to take on this huge endeavor, they were ready as always. It was just another day in the office for the men and women of the USCG. They were all ready to support the Rescue Efforts that would be staged out of Air Station New Orleans's back yard; Captain Bruce Jones and his Air Station would have the assistance of air-stations nationwide.

To use a nautical Coast Guard term, Katrina took a right turn and had "Constant Bearing and Decreasing Range" (CBDR) on her target. The Constant Bearing was her path, and her path led her right to the Louisiana/ Mississippi coastline. The Decreasing Range meant it was getting closer and closer with no thoughts of turning around. Landfall was only a matter of time. The only thing one could pray and hope for was that Katrina would decrease in strength as impact was inevitable.

Hours before landfall in the early morning of August 29, 2005, Katrina (now a Category 3 Hurricane) gave the nation a glimpse of what was to come. Storm surges started creeping up the shoreline to nearby towns, the winds picked up, and the downpour of rain commenced. No one knew exactly what was going on except for the people that were left or stayed behind. Even the national media was blinded as Katrina made landfall. There was a blackout of sorts for a brief moment in the hardest hit areas.

The impending danger was too much, even for the most skilled and well equipped.

Coast Guard Air Station New Orleans, lay desolate and unmanned as its personnel waited in nearby inland towns. They were waiting to clean up the mess that was about to occur. The helicopters and aircrews from Air Station New Orleans were evacuated and strategically placed at Coast Guard Air Station Houston. Whether the crews traveled there by helicopter or by car, they all waited patiently in the pre-determined staging area. Air Station Houston, a self-contained facility at Ellington Air Force Base, was well out of harms way and was conveniently located in a major metropolitan area with the capability of supporting this operation and supplying whatever provisions were needed. With its proximity to New Orleans, availability of maintenance personnel, facilities, and local lodging for resting aircrews, Air Station Houston became the central point for replenishment of equipment, aircrews, and maintenance of broken helicopters.

Katrina gets her way and at 0610 on the morning of August 29, 2005, she makes landfall. With an immense storm surge, she pushed out of the Gulf ripping, tearing and flooding the land. The surge swelled up and submerged swamps 30 miles inland, billions of gallons of water were driven up the Mississippi River and its tributaries. Torrential rains filled the lakes in the area to the point of overflowing. All of that water caused the saturation and provided the pressure that failed the levees along the canals and then contributed to the failure of the levee along Lake Pontchartrain. Further east into Mississippi, the catastrophic winds left their mark in history and trees bowed down from their roots while rooftops and homes took flight. Many coastal towns were completely removed from the landscape.

Just a few short hours after Katrina's initial impact, Coast Guard personnel received the green light to launch their helicopters and aircrews. The years of dedication, training and preparation were about to be put to the ultimate test. It was up to the initial responders to assess the situation for the nation and begin the rescue efforts. The first called to the task were the helicopters and aircrews from Air Station Houston and New Orleans. Crews launched from Lake Charles and Houston just hours after Katrina's impact and began assessing the situation. The rescues would come next and would last for days. The stories that follow are those of 5 Coast Guard heroes who answered when the nation called.

CHAPTER TWO

The Mighty Dauphin and her Crew

2

Acquired by the United States Coast
Guard in the early 1980's, the Dauphin
helicopter immediately started filling
its role as a short-range-recovery (SRR)
helicopter. Its sleek design, speed capability, use of composites and advanced avionics vastly changed the search and rescue business. But there is no new acquisition of a sophisticated system that ever happens without some sort of problem and the new French designed helicopter was no exception to that reality. The main limits of the Dauphin became evident early in its service with the USCG. Its size and power limitations were particularly frustrating for the crews that operated it in the field on Search and Rescue cases. It was also different than the previous helicopters the CG had procured because it could not land on the water.

In the beginning of its tour with the CG, the Dauphin was plagued with engine and avionics issues. The difference between an old dependable piece of equipment and the new one is "time in service". Time gives the pilots an opportunity to learn how to use the new bird and time gives the maintainers (mechanics) the needed practice repairing it. With the new Dauphin Helicopter, the pilots had to deal with completely new concepts. All the American designed helicopters that the CG had operated before had rotor systems that turned to the left with an open tail rotor, but the new French machines had rotor heads that turned to the right with an enclosed tail rotor with eleven blades.

Some of the differences were easy to deal with and learning the new systems was not that difficult for the pilots and crews, but not having the room for survivors or the lift capabilities of the older machines definitely took some getting used to. Now that the Dauphin has well over twenty years of service defending and saving the wonderful citizens of the United

States, it has become the old dependable helicopter. Its performance as a first response helicopter has become legendary. The Coast Guard has a unique concept with regard to aircraft maintenance that works very well and has made the CG the premier service in aviation safety and helicopter availability. The concept is called "fixers that fly".

Coast Guard aircraft are all crewed by the same people that work on them; this kind of gives the technicians a vested interest in the quality of their work. Flying in the same machine they just worked on tends to make them do a topnotch job every time. This is part of the reason that the Dauphin became such a solid performer. The CG is also in the business of saving money, so instead of buying a new helicopter to do the same job the Dauphin does, the CG has continually upgraded its helicopters with the newest technology when it becomes available. The CG also overhauls each Dauphin every three or four years depending on the environment in which it is operated. The newest version of the Dauphin is the most capable SRR helicopter to date.

Evolution has spawned a Dauphin helicopter that is capable of flying itself to any geographic point on the planet with an accuracy rate of 50 feet or less. Prior to arrival at the intended point, the helicopter determines the winds and can execute an approach oriented with a final approach course into the wind and then it can descend to a stable 50 foot hover without the pilot having to touch the controls. This type of capability drastically improves the effectiveness of the crew. There is a finite amount of tasking that can be handled by a crew, so having tools like the amazing avionics package and advanced flight director of the Dauphin helps relieve some of the constant oversight involved with flying. The automation gives the operator added capacity to manage the other challenges of a SAR case.

One thing that differentiates a CG rescue crew from every other aircraft crew in the world, including combat crews, is the weather factor. When a CG duty Aircraft Commander is told to launch on a SAR case, people's lives are in peril, weather conditions are taken into account, but not launching to save a life is a decision that is measured to the infinite degree. The visibility limits for a CG rescue helicopter are Zero-Zero. The term Zero-Zero means nothing can be seen up or straight out. Zero vertical visibility and zero horizontal visibility are the actual technical definitions. Wars are called off in weather conditions that a CG crew calls a good training day.

When a Dauphin crew launches there are four people aboard the helicopter: the Aircraft Commander, the Copilot, the Flight Mechanic and the Rescue Swimmer. Every crew position is a specialty. Each of them have hundreds and in some cases thousands of hours honing their skills. The Aircraft Commander (AC) is ultimately responsible for the lives of the crew, the lives of those he rescues and the outcome of the case whether it be good or bad. The burden on the AC is immense, and although every AC possesses the talent to accomplish the job, each time a helicopter is launched on a rescue mission the situation is different. The variables and dynamics of a case can become extremely intense very rapidly. That is why there are exhaustive training requirements, flying hour requirements and minimums before a pilot can elevate to the position of AC. Every effort is made to qualify the best AC possible. After all, lives are at stake.

An Aircraft Commander is given "the keys to the car" so to speak, when they are designated as an AC. Such fond terms like "keys to the car" and "go forth and do good things" are used to explain that this person is expected to take a ten million dollar helicopter and its crew to any given spot, in any given weather, to pluck desperate people from certain death. They are held accountable for the welfare of anyone or anything that they pickup and are scrutinized for every decision made. It is an overwhelming expectation at times, but considered part of the job and every AC embraces the weight of the responsibility.

Under-sung most times, the Co-Pilot is fondly said to be "worth their weight in fuel". As arrogant as an Aircraft Commander can be, if you catch one in a moment of soft truthfulness, he would say, "I am glad that guy was there to keep me out of trouble." The Co-Pilot could be anyone. She could be an ex-enlisted mechanic with more hours and systems knowledge in the helicopter than the AC, or he could be a complete rookie who is greener than the grass in Kentucky, but they all bring valuable knowledge to the mission.

Flight Mechanics are the link and rationale on many cases. By training, they are aircraft technicians that are beyond value assessment. The Flight Mechanic is routinely a gritty specialist who monitors the progress of the mission and provides that missing bit of information that will save the day. They bring logic and sanity in the most extreme conditions. Although outranked by his pilot, the Flight Mechanic's input is valued greatly and many times used to make the toughest of decisions. The AC relies heavily on the vast amount of systems knowledge and experience that Flight Mechanics bring to the crew.

The Rescue Swimmer is usually the hero and at times the guy in the back who keeps everyone focused. The Rescue Swimmer is invaluable, and although not directly responsible for anything during transit to or from the scene, the Rescue Swimmer hears everything that is being communicated. In many instances they can point out things that seem out of the ordinary or not in accordance with standard procedures. Once on-scene the Rescue Swimmer again has the last call as to whether or not he or she will be hoisted down to the scene. Based on experience and training, the Rescue Swimmer must take the last look and make sure that nothing has been overlooked and that the helicopter and crew are setup for success. The Rescue Swimmer is basically the last link in the Risk Management chain. Once hoisted down, the Rescue Swimmer becomes the on-scene commander and is responsible for the rescue and well being of the survivors. It's a tough job, but somebody's got to do it.

All four crew positions are crucial to the safe and efficient execution of the mission. Each position plays a different role, all are critical. It is important to note that the Coast Guard has done an outstanding job at standardizing phraseology, actions and roles. Having standard practices throughout the Coast Guard allows for versatility and safety. A pilot from Air Station Houston can fly with a Flight Mechanic from Air Station New Orleans, they can pickup a Rescue Swimmer from Air Station Miami and another Pilot from Air Station Kodiak and execute a mission as if they had been flying together all their lives. During the hundreds of Sorties flown rescuing people after Katrina, a great many of the flights were executed by mixed crews from all over the nation. The many years of stringent standardization paid off too, as is evident by the successful rescue missions flown in New Orleans. These men and women trained all their professional lives for this moment and when the time came they answered the call.

CHAPTER THREE

INSTRUCTOR PILOT
Lt. Sean O'Brien

3

All true heroes have unique stories. Although their acts of courage and bravery are what unite them at the core, it's their individual upbringings and life experiences that define who they are and how they got here. Our first interview was with a soft spoken and very humble H65 Dauphin pilot, Lieutenant Sean O'Brien. His accounts were not filled with self promoting acclaims of grandeur, just facts that would have anyone mesmerized in jaw-dropping awe at how calmly he chronicled the mass and magnitude of his time spent rescuing the helpless victims of Katrina. His story starts in Philadelphia, Pennsylvania where he was born December 20, 1974. A good Catholic family is the only way to define the O'Brien clan.

The oldest of five children born to James & Nancy O'Brien, Sean was like any other kid in the community of Havertown, a place best described as a hardworking middleclass burrow of Philadelphia. His family was fairly big by today's standards as well. He had a younger brother, Seamus and three younger sisters, Kelly, Molly and Bridget. All of them were cared for and given the solid foundations for a successful life. Their father James was a school teacher and their mother Nancy honored her family with her constant nurturing and secure home. Sean attended a Catholic Elementary School when he was a boy. Of course he got in trouble and jockeyed for position in life just like everyone else in the world, but Sean knew at an early age he had a support structure that provided him a means for success.

Sean attributes his devotion for helping people in need and his dedication to serving his country to his wholesome and humble upbringing. He gained values that were instilled in him at an early age by his parents. "I never heard my father curse" he boasted, "And my parents never missed any of their kids' sporting events." The pride he exuded about his parents was warming to the heart, a gripping feeling of something done right by these great and obviously committed parents of a humble hero. His high school years were spent at an all-boy Catholic School. Sean confessed he was not the number one student in his class. He just made good grades and had a passion for playing football. It was during his senior year that he first found out about the Coast Guard, thanks in large part to his good grades and his talents on the football field.

Raised in the city, Sean had no firsthand encounters with the sea-going service that he would eventually become an integral part of. It wasn't until he received a call from a Coast Guard Academy football recruiter that he considered a life as a Coastie. During his senior year in High School he was courted by more than a couple of prominent schools. To further complicate one of the toughest decisions an 18 year old would ever have to make, Sean's father had recently become a professor at Villanova, meaning he could attend that highly regarded University free of charge.

Sean's dilemma stemmed from the fact that he had been given a congressional appointment to attend the U.S. Naval Academy in Annapolis, MD but that's not really where his heart led him. A stipulation James and Nancy put on the kids about college was that they had to pay their own way. He could have attended Villanova as all the O'Brien kids were granted free tuition since James was a professor. But they had to pay for everything else themselves. Even with free tuition Villanova would cost a lot of money. That meant he would have to work and attend college at the same time. Then there was the University of Pennsylvania where he had also been accepted, but that would really put a burden on an already empty wallet. Obviously the financial aspect of attending college was a big concern for Sean, and attending school without a full scholarship would be a tough road to travel.

Military service was in Sean's distant past because both of his grandfathers had fought in World War II. His grandfather, James C. O'Brien, didn't just participate in World War II, he was an aviator which was something Sean had thought about doing. The Coast Guard recruiter told Sean what he wanted to hear, "You can play football and all expenses are paid." He also admits that the missions of the CG were intriguing to him. "At heart" he said, "I would rather save people than have to go to war against them." Taking all the emotional and financial variables into account, Sean decided to focus his efforts on getting into the Coast Guard Academy. As gung-ho as he was, he was not accepted on the first go-around and was placed on the waiting list until a slot opened up. Sure enough, he got the call saying there was a slot for him, and he accepted.

Getting into the Academy, as hard as it was, couldn't compare to actually making it to graduation. The first thing Sean remembered about his time at the Academy was the fact he got into great shape. He was able to maintain his peak physical conditioning the whole time he was there because he had outstanding exercise facilities and plenty of good food to eat. Living a scripted life where every moment of the day is outlined and accounted for makes a person conform. Even if someone knows what is supposed to happen, it still doesn't take away the difficulty of achieving the goals that are laid out for them. Successfully conforming means a cadet must endure a program that strips them of all individuality. Physical and mental stresses are the tools that pry all the detrimental character traits from a cadet. The arduous curriculum, military lifestyle and constant tension peal away the rough outer layers of civilian life to expose a cadet's raw inner material. Those freshly skinned and virgin cadets can then be built backup into a solid officers with uncompromising character and dedication to duty beyond measure.

Once these cadets have been commissioned into active duty officers, their common experiences of Academy life acts as the glue that bonds them together for life. "The camaraderie in my class is a lasting emotion for all of us, no matter what, I know I can count on those 158 people whenever I need them." The attrition rate for Sean's Academy class of cadets was about fifty-nine percent. Of the 380 cadets that started with him only 158 became commissioned officers in the Coast Guard. Sean admits that he was not the number one cadet academically or athletically, but he enjoyed life and learning at the Academy.

Honor, Respect and Devotion to Duty are instilled as fundamental values in every Coast Guard Officer, and putting those ideals together to become a great leader is the challenge that all of them face. Sean's journey to become a great leader began when he was assigned as an Ensign to the Coast Guard Cutter Vigorous (CGC Vigorous). Everyone has a job title and his was First Lieutenant. What that meant for Sean was a 24/7 position on a 210 foot ship that spent hundreds of days at sea every year. His primary responsibility in addition to driving the ship on a duty rotation, was the management of the deck crew, whose sole duty was to keep the ship from rusting to pieces and maintain readiness for the mission at hand. He was also expected to lead his crew and help shape their futures by setting the example and helping manage their careers.

Missions such as recovering Haitian migrants in the Caribbean or intercepting contraband smugglers in the drug infested waters off the Coast of Columbia are what Sean had to keep his ship prepared for. Meeting those types of challenges are the things that forge a leader. The truth about whether an officer is a good leader is told by those that served under that officer's command. When specifically asked about his commands on the CGC Vigorous he said, "They were great, the Executive Officer (XO is the second in command under the Captain) actually drove my medical record to Washington, DC to submit it to the flight school board." To become a pilot every officer that wants a shot at becoming an aviator has to compete with all the other qualified officers bidding for a limited number of openings at flight school. The board is actually a panel of senior officers that review every applicant's record to determine who is best qualified for the slots. Sean's XO cared enough to personally deliver his record to the board so Sean would not miss the opportunity to compete. Caring for their crew is one of those traits that develop with an officer growing into a real leader. Selfless support of their crew is the sign of a "good one". So when Sean told the story of his XO and how he admired his leadership, it was absolutely certain that his XO truly cared and set the example on how to lead the right way.

When a Coast Guard Cutter like the Vigorous leaves the dock for a patrol, it is

common for a helicopter to be assigned as an aerial asset. The helicopter and its crew become the eyes and ears for its mother-ship high above the surface. One of Sean's jobs on the ship was to act as the leader of the fire fighting crew that provided the safety measures for every helicopter takeoff and landing. It was his close interaction with the helicopter and its crew that prompted Sean to make the pivotal decision to apply for flight school. Sean smiled when he said, "In one week that helicopter crew got a drug bust, used the helicopter to MEDEVAC (medical evacuation) one of the ship's crew and they even conducted a SAR case… that is what really made my decision for me."

Sean was one of the lucky ones; he was accepted to flight school on his first try. There are several other people he knew that had to apply more than once and one in particular applied 5 times. Sean counted his blessings and shared the news with his wife Valerie. Val, the woman he calls his biggest cheerleader, was excited for him and knew he had worked hard to earn this great opportunity. However, when the proposition of moving to a completely new part of the country to participate in an extremely difficult program that fails half its candidates is presented, it takes some serious contemplation. They discussed the decision a little, but there really was no indecision on either part. As far as they were both concerned, they were ready to go, regardless of the sacrifices this stringent training program would put on both of them.

Naval Flight training takes place in Pensacola, Florida. Entering the gates of Naval Air Station Pensacola there is a sign that reads "Welcome to the Cradle of Naval Aviation", which kind of says it all. It is not so much boasting, but a simple fact. The men and women that complete the training and become designated "Naval Aviators" are truly the best pilots in the world. The course is so auspicious that foreign governments (allies) send their elite candidates to take the challenge of the intense U.S. program. If the exchange pilots are successful, they take back talents and unparalleled fundamental aviation abilities to be used in the defense of their home countries. If you do not believe that Navy trained pilots are the best in the world, just ask one and they will tell you.

When asked about flight school, every Naval Aviator will have a different story to tell. When asked if they had any difficulties making it through the training, the honest ones will say yes. The program is designed to find a candidate's weakness; for Sean that would be his inability to float. What he meant was that when required to tread water for five minutes wearing a helmet, flight suit, boots and sporting a vest that has been weighted down with lead, he tends to sink.

Sean explained, "I can swim great, it was swimming a mile in flight gear that was difficult." Some people cope better than others and some people can not cope at all. The ones that can't cope get an opportunity to fly a desk.

Sean completed Flight Training with no real problems. He put in the time and was sharp enough to meet all requirements to earn his "Wings of Gold". On graduation day Sean got all dressed up, and he and his wife went to his Winging Ceremony, an event that culminated what he calls "… the toughest time of my life, but when it was over I was proud to know that I was able to make it." Another pleasant surprise that occurred around the same time was that Sean and Valerie were expecting their first child. Conor would be born a few months after they transferred to their first Air Station.

Assignments to fill pilot positions in the CG are based on the "needs of the service", which means, a pilot goes where the Guard tells them to go. Sean was needed to fill a position in Traverse City, Michigan. Putting it in CG terms, Sean's first duty station as a pilot was Air Station Traverse City. Northern stations are not enjoyed by every pilot, but Sean and his family were accustomed to the cold weather and made Michigan their home for the next four years. Sean told stories of rescuing stranded mariners from the frozen waters of Lake Michigan after launching his helicopter into weather that neither a man nor beast in their right mind would think about flying in. "Those zero visibility and zero temperature conditions were normal operations for the crew of Traverse City", it was business as usual and all they knew.

On one case Sean recalled, he had launched on the crappiest of crappy days in hopes of finding some guys that had taken a homemade hovercraft onto the frozen surface of Lake Winnebago and never returned. It happened to be New Year's Eve and the weather, forget about it, it was thicker and colder than slush; it was like flying in a frozen margarita from his story. Sean flew the helicopter at 200 feet above the ice in near zero visibility until finally finding the half frozen adventurers clinging to the remains of a shattered vessel. The under engineered craft had struck a mini iceberg and had broken in half before sinking through the ice. He didn't know it at the time, but the local volunteer fire department had setout to find the same unlucky joy riders with one of their hovercraft. After picking up the backyard boat builders he found out that almost the same thing had happened to the would-be rescuers from the fire department.

Since the first rescue had gone well and everybody was safe there was no reason the next case should be much different, he thought. The thing about pilots is that the young ones never say, "Don't do what I did," they always say, "Let's just go and get it done." The moral of that story is, there are old pilots and there are bold pilots, but there are very few old-bold pilots. A pilot becomes old by learning from the mistakes they make that don't kill them. That day Sean learned that water blown up from the surface of a freshwater lake, in freezing temperatures, becomes ice when it comes in contact with a helicopter hovering in that type of wet environment. Ice drastically affects the aerodynamics of an aircraft in flight. "I was hovering and the helicopter started to become heavy and the instruments started freezing up. I didn't realize it for a few seconds but the whole aircraft had a sheet of ice building on it. We got the survivors into the helicopter just in time because as I climbed out, gaining altitude, the ice started shedding from the rotor blades and we started gaining lift which allowed us to fly out safely."

Pilots call stories like that one "lessons learned". The stories that have a bad outcome are called incidences and sometimes accidents. Those are the stories of crashes, broken helicopters and injuries. Sean has many lessons learned which makes him a seasoned aviator, one that has the experience to handle a complex mission, managing all the variables to get the best outcome possible for his crew and the people he is sent to save.

Their tour in Traverse City was an adventure for both Valerie and Sean, one that they will cherish forever. During their four years in Michigan they had their first son Conor, their second child Michael and discovered something about Conor that would impact their family forever. As it turned out, their oldest son Conor was diagnosed with Autism. It is something that Sean and Valerie freely discuss and a topic that Sean was comfortable sharing with this book. In Sean's opinion, he knows that talking about Autism is the only way to raise the aware-ness for those that do not know about it. Sharing Conor's story in this book also exemplifies how the Coast Guard takes care of its people. Conor has a special need that the CG acknowledges. When the time came to move to a new duty station, medical care in the area was a factor in where the O'Briens would be transferred. The CG motto is that if your family isn't taken care of then you can't possibly be of any use to the service or the people it serves.

In June 2004, after all things were considered, Sean and Valerie packed up with Conor and Michael and then set off for Coast Guard Air Station Houston, Texas. By that time Sean had become a specialist within the Aviation Field as

an Aviation Safety Officer. He attended all the requisite courses at the University of Southern California earning a Masters Certificate in Engineering Safety and Security. The USC program satisfied the requirements for the unique field of expertise. His new job in Houston would be one of a department head in charge of the Aviation Safety program. Sean would also become one of the instructor pilots tasked with the molding of the next generation of Coast Guard rescue pilots.

A year went by with Sean and Valerie learning the area and setting up a home. Conor got established with his doctors, the kids got accustomed to new schools and things started to stabilize for them; stable enough in fact that soon after ar-

riving in Houston, Sean and Valerie were expecting their 3rd son Jack. Military families start over every four years (or less) with new communities, friends and challenges. The public sees the praise a military member receives for their heroism and sacrifices, but what most people aren't aware of is the toll that type of life takes on the members' families. People like Valerie and the thousands of other spouses, children and parents of military members live life everyday worrying about their loved ones. Sean spoke about Valerie, "Val is the best, I think she tries not to think about how dangerous the job is and she supports me one hundred percent."

Who would have known that in August of 2005 an angry storm named Katrina would test our nation's strength, as well as Val's fortitude and Sean's individual skills and courage. By then Sean was set as one of the senior Lieutenants at Air Station Houston and held the position and responsibility of Senior Duty Officer (SDO). The SDO of any CG Air Station is in charge of every aspect of operating the unit and expected to make the right decisions during their twenty-four hour duty cycle. An SDO acts on behalf of the Commanding Officer (CO) making every decision and processing every case. It is a huge responsibility that these brilliant individuals handle as smoothly as buying a candy bar at the corner store.

Everyday of every year there are thousands of duty officers from every branch of the military that provide a concise synopsis of the world and how their individual unit fits into the current condition of the globe. The CG calls it "The Brief". When Katrina entered the Gulf of Mexico and the probability that she would strike the Gulf Coast increased, Sean remembered briefing his command on the track and predicted strike area. Part of the brief for a significant event like a Category 5 hurricane is preparedness. In other words how prepared is the unit, what is the plan for evacuation, where are key personnel and what will be the unit's response for the relief effort. All of these elements of readiness are continually evaluated until each action is put into play.

As Katrina neared landfall, the established plan of action was executed by all the units along the Gulf. As a member of the Coast Guard each Coastie has about 36,000 people that they consider family. When Katrina narrowed her focus on Louisiana and Mississippi the evacuations started. Families that fled from those areas dispersed in all directions and some of them came to Houston. Many of them stayed with family, Coast Guard family. The O'Briens received friends and unknown Coasties from Air Station New Orleans. In many cases the host families did not know the people they took into their homes on a personal level, but they were all welcomed with open arms because that is the Coast Guard way.

The night of August 28, 2005 Sean went out to dinner with friends that had evacuated in hopes of avoiding Katrina. The guys told sea-stories and caught up on what they had been doing in their own lives. It was a casual evening with them talking about how things might turn out and what their units had been through in the last few days with Katrina's approach. But, having dinner that night in Houston, watching Katrina barrel toward Louisiana on the television, they never imagined that the next few days would bring events so destructive and epic to their part of the country that an indelible mark would be left on the United States. They had no idea that issues like politics, racism, global warming, ineptitude, heroism, life and death were about to be a significant part of their lives in the hours and days to come.

6:10 am on August 29th, Hurricane Katrina made landfall and history. She had diminished to a category three storm by that time, but that didn't mean much to the impact zone. Along the coast of Eastern Louisiana and Western Mississippi structures like homes, buildings, roads, towers and bridges were completely blown apart. Their components and shattered pieces were shredded and then relocated to places miles away. Huge casino barges were lifted like toy boats in the surf by the storm surge, breaking them from their concrete moorings and carrying them inland. The majority of the coastal residents had taken warning when the evacuation was announced, sparing the families that resided so close to shore. Katrina mercilessly assaulted the coast leaving cataclysmic devastation in her wake.

First to witness the aftermath in the impact zone were Coasties that had waited only long enough to shadow Katrina's backside. Helicopter crews from Texas, Alabama, Florida and North Carolina followed close behind in her strong gale-force storms. The helicopter crews started the initial assessment for a nation that was holding its breath. They also began rescue efforts immediately, and although their initial tasking was to assess the area, instincts took over and they starting pulling survivors out of harms way.

Sean was not part of the first wave of helicopters to reach the scene, his time to shine came about forty-eight hours after landfall. He spent the hours immediately after Katrina's storm passage supporting the overwhelming task of organizing the first response and preparing for the second wave. To keep a helicopter in action around the clock requires multiple crews. Even super-heroes get fatigued and adrenaline can only carry one so far. Additionally, there are those pesky regulations about mandatory rest that keep even the biggest and boldest heroes on the ground for a few hours. Sean's job was to relieve the first wave pilots for the mop-up, but who knew the Lake Pontchartrain levies would break and bring a deluge to the already devastated city.

On the morning of August 31, 2005, Sean assembled his crew and departed Houston for New Orleans. When they arrived there was no semblance of order. Helicopters were buzzing over the city like wasps over a nest. There was no air traffic control and calls for rescues were streaming over the radios continuously. Sean described the seen as "unbelievable, it was a massive bowl of water and humanity, people were everywhere and they all wanted help." Sean remembers thinking to himself, "Oh shit! What are we getting into? I didn't expect this." He also recalls being excited and "a little bit fired-up," during the first couple of sorties he flew while in support of this tremendous rescue effort.

The crew's first rescue was a family of six. When Sean's crew spotted the family, they were in chest-high water pushing their five year old son on an inflatable raft down the street. The unfortunate family had been in the water for approximately twenty hours at the point before they were plucked from the putrid stew of chemicals and sewage. "We just kept on going after that," Sean explained. "It was one hoist after the other, for hours all we did was fly from rooftop to rooftop picking people up and taking them to high ground."

Coast Guard helicopter pilots are especially proficient at flying in extreme weather and finding desperate people on the open water, but urban rescues are not the norm for these skilled aviators. Obstacles such as power lines, towers and huge trees add a different dimension to rescues in a metropolitan area like New Orleans. Sean described many situations where he had to hover his helicopter between trees and power lines that were a few feet away from his rotor, and when we say a few feet we mean extremely close. This type of confined area hoisting became the "norm" rather quickly. Another significant complication was the amount of helicopter traffic and the lack of communication amongst the aircraft in the area. The sky above the "scene" was congested with rescue helicopters from many different agencies. There were also pesky media helicopters that added to the danger of a midair collision.

Challenging situations are oddly the fuel that these unique individuals thrive on. As their first day went on, the crew formed a solid team that communicated intuitively. Training and thousands of hours of practice provided them a script for success that played out over and over as they plucked victim after victim from dire straights. Sean and his crew, like all Coasties, are the people that turn chaos into a workable situation and come out with lives saved. In one twenty-four hour period Sean's crew saved 110 lives. That is more than most Coast Guard pilots will save in a 20 year career.

Stories that were told only by those that were rescued alarmed the crews as they found out the horrible situations these destitute people had been faced with. In some cases gangs had confiscated the relief provisions that had been dropped for the victims. There were stories of gangs that horded food and water from children and women who truly needed the supplies to survive. The gangs used intimidation and muscle to keep

the provisions solely for themselves. One event that Sean described was hoisting-up a man in his early twenties from a rooftop. When the man was brought into the helicopter, Matt Bone, the flight mechanic, informed Sean that the man had a pistol in his belt. Sean told Matt, "Don't make a big deal about the gun, we will just take him to the evacuation area and get him out of the helicopter. Then we will inform the authorities on the ground about the pistol." This happened more than once during his crews rescue efforts. It was an inevitable situation that was bound to happen because high concentrations of the rescues were in high crime areas.

Hoisting to apartment buildings provides a particularly unique challenge for the crews. In the absence of a flat or slightly angled area like a rooftop, the crews had to improvise their techniques for getting the Rescue Swimmer to the survivors through a window. These types of hoists are considered a "vertical surface deployment". Although trained in the technique, it is not common and impromptu methods are developed to get the job done. Sean had to swing the swimmer back and forth using the helicopter, and when the swimmer had enough swing to make contact he would have to grab anything he could to hold on to the building. The agile rescuer would then have to traverse to the open window and climb in and release from the rescue hook to assess the situation on-scene.

Hour after hour the crew saved as many as they possibly could. Rally points were setup on any spot of high ground clear enough to land a chopper. Lake Front Airport was one of those places. Sean remembers seeing thousands of people along the runways waiting for the next leg of their passage to safety, a place where they could get the minimum basic needs. Other drop-off points were freeway overpasses and the Super Dome. For rescuers the immediate removal of victims from life threatening situations is the objective. In other words, getting the victims high-and-dry was the number one goal.

Night took away the light and added a dimension of terror for the victims. It also made the rescues more risky for the CG aircrews, especially the rescue swimmer. Sean has great admiration for these specialized and selfless individuals. He explained how the lack of electricity and the desperation of the people below make it difficult for the swimmers. "I feel for those guys, I would drop my swimmer off in a building and he didn't know what or who was in there. Having no lights and with the people being terribly desperate, I was really concerned for his safety. Many times we had to leave him on-scene while we took the folks he sent up back to safety. These dudes do a fantastic job and the country should know more about them."

Late on their first night in New Orleans was when Sean earned the United States Air Medal and his rescue swimmer earned the Distinguished Flying Cross for their heroic efforts. Throughout the day many helicopters had been flying the same path to Lake Front Airport. Along that path was an elderly couple standing on their rooftop. Sean had seen them a couple of times, but didn't have the fuel or space to rescue them, and they seemed secure enough, or at least they were not in any eminent danger. After night fall the crew was bringing back some survivors to Lake Front when they saw the couple again only this time the house next to the one they were standing on was ablaze. Sean remembers that he felt it was his duty to get these folks off immediately! The only problem was that the area the helicopter needed to be positioned for the hoist was below some large oak trees and next too some power lines. Not only that, but the helicopter needed to hover between the inferno and the old folks' house; now that's being stuck between a rock and hard place.

Embers from the fire next door were blowing directly on the house where the old folks were standing. To further complicate things, Sean's co-pilot was violently throwing up next to him. The smoke and fumes coming up from the burning house only made matters worse for the poor guy. Sean said, "I really gotta hand it to him though, he never gave up. He puked in his flight glove then handed it back to the flight mechanic who through it out the cockpit, then he would go back to making radio calls and calling out my obstacles. He was a heck of a trooper." Regardless of the sick co-pilot, flames, blistering heat and low fuel scenario, Sean had a job to do. He put his helicopter right where it needed to be below the trees, in between the power lines and next to the fire.

Hoisting the couple was a bit tricky because of all the obstacles that lay in the way, but these guys know their stuff and the evolution went smoothly. The two survivors were taken to the airport and handed off to the ground crews for triage. The next day Sean's crew flew over the house they had hoisted from only hours before and found it completely burned. Sean is certain, if the old folks were on that roof top any longer, help could not have reached them and they would have perished.

"In this business, on the spot decisions are the reason people live to see another day. In this case I am absolutely certain that we made the difference between these people surviving Katrina and not. A whole family was affected. These folks have brothers, sisters, children and grandchildren that could have lost their loved ones if we weren't there at that particular moment. Praise is not why we do the job, it's the satisfaction of saving a life that makes everything we do, day-to-day, worth while. It is my duty to serve the American public and help them sleep a little easier knowing that we are here to help if they need us." As humble as that sounds, you could sense great pride as Sean described this rescue story and many others. Although most Coast Guard pilots you come across are modest individuals, the work they do is extremely dangerous and requires tons of courage.

For the average American it is hard to comprehend what these brave men and women go through to become the best rescuers in the world. Maybe this book will help inform the public about a very unique and specialized branch of the Armed Services. The Coast Guard is now a member of the Department of Homeland Security were it will take a lead role in securing our country from terrorism along with being the first responders during horrible catastrophies like Hurricane Katrina. Sean and his crew saved a total of 224 lives from the storms aftermath, that's 224 people that had no other way out. If you run into one of these heroes, make sure to say thanks.

RESCUE SWIMMER
AST3 Charles Medema

4

It's amazing how things happen sometimes. Our heroes all have innate abilities and drive to be the best. They all
use their special skills and talents to save
others, but for AST3 Charles Medema,
it was all about being at the right place at the right time. Charles, also
known as "Funky Chuck Medema", was the newest AST stationed at
Coast Guard Air Station Houston, serving just miles away from his childhood hometown of Baytown, TX. He lived in Baytown all his life with his
mom, Ruth and his stepfather, Mike LaValley. Chuck was born to swim so
it's not hard understanding how he excelled in Swimming and Water Polo
at Baytown High School.

Following High School graduation, Chuck worked as a lifeguard while he
figured out what he wanted to do with his life. The only thing he really
knew for sure was that college wasn't the right thing for him at that time.
Once the summer ended, his lifeguard job ended as well. Not knowing
what he was going to do for money, he decided to give the Navy a shot, after all "The Navy might be a place for me while I find something better to
do." It was a simple process once he made the final decision to join. He
went down to the recruiting office, signed the enlistment papers, and three
days later he was in Navy Boot Camp.

Chuck did well in Boot Camp, quickly realizing that all the yelling,
screaming, pushups, and running were just part of the program. One way
or another, this would be good for him, he knew it. Graduation day was a
proud day for Chuck. This was the first really big accomplishment of his
adult life, and it was a step in the right direction for whatever the future
might hold for him. With Boot Camp in the rear-view mirror, his specialty
training was next. Slated to serve the Navy as an Aviation Boatswain's
Mate, he would have to attend more school.

Aviation Boatswain's Mate school was tough. He spent long days learning about aircraft servicing, handling and the hazards associated with the powerful and extremely dangerous machines. The safety part of the training was vitally important for him to grasp as aircraft handling is an unforgiving business and takes many lives every year. Once he completed school, Chuck received orders to his first duty station. He was destined to spend the next few years of his life as an Aviation Boatswain's Mate onboard the USS Enterprise. His job would be handling aircraft in the most dynamic environment imaginable.

The flight deck of a nuclear powered aircraft carrier such as the one on the USS Enterprise is many times referred to as "The Most Dangerous Quarter Mile on the Planet." One false move and a Navy man can go from "squid" to hamburger meat in a split second. Aircraft carrier flight decks are a place where every single action is choreographed and accounted for in an attempt to mitigate some of the risks and hazards involved. Chuck remembers several bad days, "Yeah, I saw two guys get killed. One got sucked into a Jet Engine. The second guy walked into a propeller. These are definitely bad memories and that was a very stressful and scary environment to work in."

One positive aspect of Chuck's Navy service was that he got to see Navy Rescue Swimmers in action. Their job always intrigued him and captivated his imagination. As he learned more and more about what a Rescue Swimmer did, it made him want to become one himself.

The USS Enterprise, home ported in Norfolk, VA, is a massive ship. With her nuclear power plant and self-contained functionality, she could be underway for years if that were required of her. Typically when she left the dock, she could be expected to stay out for at least six months, however a cruise sometimes lasted a year or more. That's one of the biggest factors that drove Chuck out of the Navy, he didn't want to spend the rest of his life underway on a floating Navy city dodging death on a daily basis. He didn't want to miss out on life anymore, and he was tired of not being able to talk to his friends and family. Navy life is tough on a family and Chuck was just tired of leaving for months at a time, so he left the Navy at the end of his enlistment. He spent six months out of the Navy before actually considering the thought of getting back in. "Now that I look back, the Navy wasn't that bad and the pay was okay. The nicest thing is that my medical was taken care of and that my paycheck was deposited twice a month every month." Luckily for Chuck he had been doing a little career researching and found out that the Navy wasn't the only military service that had Rescue Swimmers.

Although he didn't know much about the Coast Guard, the little Chuck knew was enough to convince him that it was a better fit for him than the Navy. He found the Coast Guard's Rescue Swimmer program even more intriguing than the Navy program he had witnessed first hand. The more he read about the Coast Guard, the more he fell in love with its missions, its people and its humanitarian side. He liked it so much that he actually began the enlistment process and prepared himself for a new life. The Navy had not been all bad. He had some good times and made some good friends. He even has a lot of respect for the job they do. The Navy actually gets credit for one of the most significant moments in Chuck's life. It was the Navy's decision to send him to the Norfolk, VA that led Chuck to meet his wife. While stationed in Norfolk, Chuck came across a quiet and beautiful young lady named Jessica. "I guess the Navy was good for something. I would've never met Jessica otherwise."

In a short time frame Chuck went through two life changing events, he changed careers and decided to marry Jessica. His career change was enlisting in the Coast Guard. Even before departing for Boot Camp he had been informed that his first duty station as a Coastie would be in Louisiana. About two weeks before leaving for boot camp Chuck and Jessica were married. Chuck left for "mini Boot Camp". This was a four week program designed to assimilate prior military service members from other services into the Coast Guard. It's not as tough and not designed to "weed out" bad seeds, instead it serves to teach prior service members about the Coast Guard, its history and its missions. At mini Boot Camp Chuck and his classmates learned about the Coast Guard's ranks and rates, types of ships and cutters, its missions and roles, aircraft types and, of course, the Core Values of Honor, Respect, and Devotion to Duty.

Only having to spend four weeks in Cape May, NJ versus the eight weeks that the full Boot Camp takes, made the Navy seem a little more useful once more; after all, it got him out of four weeks of Coast Guard Boot Camp. After completing the short program, Chuck returned to Jessica so the two could pack up their things and move to Venice, LA, their first

Coast Guard duty station. Coast Guard Station Venice is about as far south in Louisiana as anyone can travel, literally hanging out into the Gulf of Mexico. The unit was placed there for quick response to boaters that get into trouble in the Gulf. The only downside to the station was that Chuck and the other crewmembers had to commute 70 miles each way to and from work. No Coastie in their right mind would live that far away from work, but Station Ven- ice was literally located in the middle of nowhere. There wasn't really any- where to live and the govern- ment housing was at the Naval Base in New Orleans. Not having any other choice, Chuck and Jessica lived on base and Chuck made the 140 mile roundtrip to work.

At his new duty station, Chuck had to do all the things that new Coasties at a small boat station must. He cleaned toilets, mopped floors and was basically treated like a servant, as all newcomers are for a little while. It makes a person appreciate the better jobs after they have washed the laundry and did the dishes for the entire crew. That fact came out when Chuck talked about his job at Air Station New Orleans, he said, "I was really glad to leave the station for the Airman Program." That wasn't all that im- proved in Chuck's life when he joined the Airman Program. His commute also changed from 140 miles roundtrip to about 5. Ironically enough, Sta- tion Venice no longer exists. It was removed from active duty by a nasty little storm named Katrina. Station Venice was only 15 miles from where Hurricane Katrina made landfall and didn't stand a chance. The station didn't make it as every part of it was ravaged by the winds and rain from

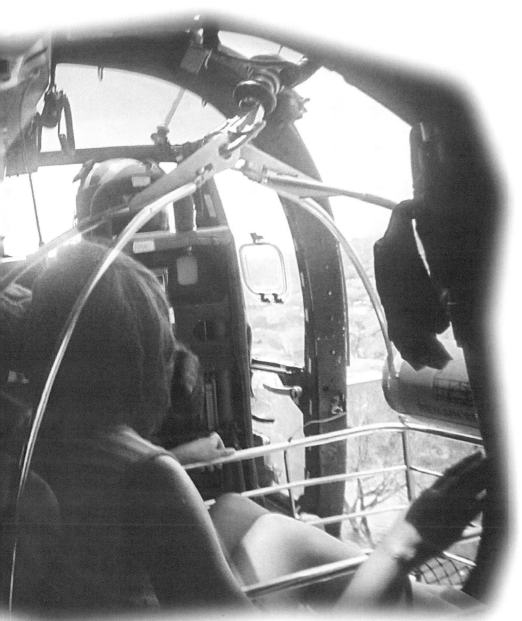

Katrina. Like many parts of Louisiana and Mississippi, Station Venice was helpless to the devastation of Hurricane Katrina.

While at Station Venice, Chuck had several significant moments. It was during his tour here that he qualified for and was accepted into the Airman Program as a future Aviation Survival Technician (AST) School candidate.

More significant however was the birth of his son Bryce. Bryce added a new dimension to their lives. They now had to care for someone else's well being and every need, but to Chuck and Jessica it was a total blessing. It was at this moment in his life that Chuck realized how truly lucky he was to be in the Coast Guard. Although he would miss some birthdays, graduations, anniversaries, and first steps, had he still been in the Navy, he could've counted on missing many more significant family events. The Coast Guard and all branches of the military do a great job of taking care of your family, they don't however guarantee that you're going to be around very much. Chuck considered himself lucky to be present for his son's birth.

Duty called soon after Bryce came along, and Chuck was told he would transfer to Coast Guard Air Station New Orleans to start the Airman Program prior to attending AST "A" School. The Airman Program, by design, gives new aviation candidates, whether they want to be mechanics, electronics experts or swimmers, a chance to learn about the aviation community, its aircraft and its people. The aviation community within the Coast Guard is very different than others, so the Airman Program serves as an experience and adjustment period. Already familiar with the aviation side of the house from his previous experience in the Navy, Chuck was able to focus on the physical fitness requirements of AST "A" School. Oddly enough however, it wasn't the physical requirements of AST "A" School that provided the biggest challenges for him.

Finally completing the Airman Program and doing his time in New Orleans, Chuck got his chance and left for Elizabeth City, NC to the Aviation Technical Training Center. This is the place he would call home for the next nineteen weeks and it would be the place where he would learn the basics of his new rate. The Aviation Technical Training Center is where all aviation enlisted personnel get their initial training. "A School was definitely the most physically and mentally challenging time of my life by a long shot. I know other aviation specialties are also tough, but I don't think any of them go through the physical challenges we go through."

Swimming, then running followed by more swimming and running was the name of the game. Not just routine running and swimming, but running with gear and swimming while pushing a brick. Every part of their training was to prepare them for the dangers they would face in the sea.

The grand prize for those lucky and skilled enough to win this game was a rewarding life full of danger and joy. What does the loser get? An all expense paid trip back to where they came from. The training seeks to bring out an individual's weakness, and many candidates fail to meet the challenging environment. Some can't swim long enough, some can't run long enough and some can't stay out of trouble. One way or another, half of the class doesn't make it through to see graduation day.

For "Funky Chuck" trouble almost got to him. He could swim just fine, even with four instructors trying to drown him. He could also run as far as they asked him too. And as far as pushups and pull-ups were concerned, forget about it. Although he wouldn't elaborate much on this topic, he did say "I thought I would handle stress a little better than I did. To be honest with you, the toughest part about "A" school was keeping out of trouble and not getting the instructors mad at me all the time." We would've expected an older and more mature individual like Chuck to handle the stresses of intense training better because of his years in the Navy. It also seems logical that the two Boot Camps would have prepared him better. The problem was that being older but still being treated like a young, good for nothing recruit can put even the best of them to the ultimate test. "Physically I didn't run into anything I couldn't do. The hard part was having to do my best and perform these physical feats everyday for 19 weeks."

There was some relief and a way to re-focus on the goal at hand. While he was attending "A" School in North Carolina, Jessica and Bryce were staying with Jessica's parents in Williamsburg, VA, which was only an hour and a half north from Elizabeth City, NC. This allowed Chuck to get away for weekends and be with his wife and son. This time away re-energized him and allowed him to focus on what was important; making it through this training to make a better life for his family. The time away gave him perspective on who he was doing this for, after all it wasn't just him anymore, and he had two other people to think about. Chuck eventually would graduate. In the end he was one of five students to graduate in a class that began with twelve candidates.

Following graduation, Chuck received orders to Coast Guard Air Station Houston. He was excited at the opportunity to serve the nation in his hometown. He would be able to visit with his family and reunite with old friends, but more importantly, his Mom would get to spend plenty of time with Bryce. Chuck and Jessica packed up once more and made their way to Houston, TX, arriving in April of 2005.

Coast Guard Air Station Houston is one of those small little Air Stations that can be considered a showplace. They have a very high up-tempo SAR schedule, but the crew is small enough to manage, and the facility is still fairly new and well maintained and funded compared to other units. The office spaces are constantly repainted and re-carpeted, all the furniture is fairly knew, and the hangar floor is immaculately kept and repainted often. Air Station Houston is a relatively smaller station with four Dauphin helicopters and a fairly junior Commander Officer that holds the rank of Commander (O-5) who many times gets promoted to Captain during his tour in Houston. Larger Air Stations with more people, aircraft and responsibility have more senior Commanding Officers that hold the rank of Captain (O-6). It was definitely a cozy place for the newest AST3 to start his career. Chuck and his family moved into an apartment and setup a home, at least until the Coast Guard decided that he needed to go somewhere else.

Immediately after completing his check-in sheet which takes a couple of days, Chuck began his training to become a qualified Rescue Swimmer. AST "A" School provides the basics and the foundation, but he had to complete the unit syllabus and get out there in the real conditions and prove himself. All new swimmers need to gain the experience and confidence that will pull them through the toughest of times. It took Chuck a while to become a qualified Rescue Swimmer, but not because he couldn't hack it, but because of the unavailability of Emergency Medical Technician (EMT) School. This is one of the schools that are required. Every Rescue Swimmer must be a qualified EMT. The school opened up, so he finally got to go. He successfully completed EMT school and returned to Houston in early August. Now all Chuck had left was his final flight before he would be fully qualified to perform his duties. This is what's called a "check ride". It's the last flight, and is used to determine if an individual is ready or not. Due to aircraft maintenance and flight scheduling issues, he had to wait until August 26, 2005 to complete his check ride. That was the Friday before Hurricane Katrina hit.

Although he had completed his syllabus and passed everything with flying colors, Chuck would not officially be a Rescue Swimmer until his Commanding Officer designated him a swimmer in writing. It is the final-final part of the designation process and is a big deal, because that is when a crewman gets their wings. The typical designation letter is presented to a new Rescue Swimmer in an official ceremony where the unit gets in formation to bear witness. The Commanding Officer has the qualification letter read out loud for all to hear. The CO then pins on the newly designated Swimmer's wings and gives him the letter, pictures are taken of the event for posterity. There may be a few kind words said and then halleluiah a new crewman is born….but not Funky Chuck, no way, he had to make a little history. A pilot, especially pilots that fly fixed wing aircraft, will probably never get the prestigious Air Medal pinned upon their chest. Only a small percent of helicopter pilots ever see them, it's pretty rare for a flight mechanic to get one too; the odds are just against it. Chuck happened to earn an Air Medal the first day on his first case as a qualified Rescue Swimmer, how is that for being in the right place at the right time?

Most members at Air Station Houston knew that all hell was going to break loose after Hurricane Katrina made landfall. Helicopters, aircrews, and evacuees had been arriving all weekend from Louisiana prior to hurricane impact. Evacuation routes were completely congested, and the normal five hour drive from New Orleans to Houston was taking close to twenty hours. The interstates were jammed and people were panicking. Calmly, the rescue aircrews waited as the world around them got more and more chaotic. Chuck had no idea that he was the first available swimmer that could deploy, heck he had just finished his "check ride" two days before and CDR Schweizer (his CO) hadn't even presented him his letter yet. That was all irrelevant. Sunday night Chuck got the call while he and his family were at his mom's house celebrating Bryce's birthday. "Pack a small bag and be here first thing in the morning. You're going on the first helicopter out to New Orleans."

The next morning Chuck woke up early and left for the air station. It was a frenzied scene but organized and purposeful. Coasties sometimes get in a rush as the adrenaline takes over, but they are always in control and have the end goal in mind. Chuck was ready to go, with or without a signed letter, after all he was ordered to go. He asked about his letter and was told not to worry about it, that it would be taken care of. Chuck went on to meet up with his crew which included Brian Crook, a real go-getter and experienced Flight Mechanic who was on the fast track to becoming an of-

ficer in the future. They packed up their things and once the pilots showed up, headed to the flight line. Chuck still did not have a signed designation letter.

On the way over, LT Smith, the Aircraft Commander, received a radio transmission stating that Chuck's letter had been signed by the CO, so he was good-to-go. Chuck had never stood duty as a Rescue Swimmer, he had never been on a live case, his letter was signed that day, nevertheless he was ready. His crew safely made it to the New Orleans area and commenced their mission. Being one of the first helicopters on scene, their primary duty was to survey the area, assess the situation and report back to the Air Station New Orleans duty desk which was now manned. The two New Orleans helicopters they followed over were tasked with the same mission. The goal was to get a quick and thorough assessment and see if there were enough resources on hand to rescue any survivors. It became obvious immediately that three or four helicopters weren't going to be enough and that these crews would be deployed for days if not weeks rescuing people. After surveying the area on their first sortie, they refueled at Coast Guard Air Station New Orleans and headed back to start rescuing survivors. This was all new to Chuck heck, his letter was just signed that day.

Chuck had lived in New Orleans rather recently, so he had a particularly keen reference of the city before and after Hurricane Katrina hit. He saw that the canal levees had already breached and that a large part of the city was under water. One thing about a Coastie, they always remember their first rescue, as does Chuck. The first survivors the crew came across were a family of six on a rooftop of a two-story house. The first person they hoisted up was a seven year old little blond headed girl. They then went on to pick up the rest of her family and brought them to the Belle Chasse Football Stadium. For the rest of the afternoon and evening it was just one rescue after another. The first day of rescues found people that were in need, but it would be nothing compared to the desperation that would become a reality a week later after the effects of heat exposure, dehydration, isolation and helplessness set in on these survivors. They picked up people from rooftops, out of the filthy water, from windows, balconies and buildings with flat roofs.

Without electricity, the city of New Orleans was pitch-black at night. The only lights visible were lighters, candles and flashlights that people were using as signaling devices in an attempt to get help. Thousands upon thousands were stranded and now it was night time, and they were all scared and wanted to be rescued at the same time. The amount of rescues was overwhelming and flying at night with no visual cues was exhausting. Chuck's crew eventually flew into "the Bag", meaning they were no longer allowed to keep flying without a waiver granted by the Operational Commander. On their way back to Air Station New Orleans they saw two men in a boat and decided to go ahead and pick these guys up on the way home. It turned out that it wouldn't be that simple.

LT Smith brought the helicopter into a hover and sent Chuck down to a rooftop close to the two men. When he finally made it down, Chuck unhooked from the hoist cable and began investigating what was going on. The men informed him that their grandmother was floating on an air mattress with life support equipment attached to her. They tried to get her on the boat but were unsuccessful. The men also informed Chuck that their mother was trapped in the house by high water. The scene was obviously a little more complicated than they had anticipated and was getting more complicated by the second. Realizing that the helicopter was low on fuel to begin with, Chuck radioed in and explained the situation. Chuck and his pilots determined that the best course of action was for Chuck to stay on scene with the survivors and for the helicopter to return to base, refuel and get authorization to fly one more sortie to pick up Chuck and the survivors.

Chuck knew this was the right decision, after all, they were here to save lives. It wouldn't be right to let this woman die just because they needed a waiver to keep flying. He was sure that the people in charge would make the right call, and they did. After the helicopter left, Chuck began preparing the scene for the rescue of these survivors. The two men seemed okay so he went on to check on the grandmother. She seemed to be stable, so he went to find the mother that was trapped inside the house. It may sound odd, but Chuck swam around the two story house in an attempt to hear the mother. When he found her through a second story window, she told him she couldn't swim. That probably explains why she stayed in the house, but regardless, Chuck had to get her out of there.

He convinced the lady to come out in the water. He assured her that he would grab hold of her and not let her go. Chuck finally got a hold of her and preceded to "buddy-tow" her back around the house to join the rest of the family and wait for the helicopter's return. Chuck now had everyone together for the hoist, if only LT Smith could convince the Operational Commander to grant an extension, they would be back in business. Just as he thought that he heard the helicopter overhead. It must not have been that tough of a decision to make for the guys back at the Air Station.

Typically, the grandmother would be sent up via a rescue basket or litter, but with all the equipment she was attached to this would not be possible. The only way he would be able to get her up into the helicopter was to perform a "Double Lift" pickup. Chuck had seen this done and even practiced it during his syllabus, but doing it for real and with all these variables would test his true skill. He took two strops and wrapped them and a blanket as securely as he could around the grandmother, then he secured the life support equipment to the rig. Next he hooked her up to himself and then the whole system he hooked to the hoist and prayed to God it worked and nothing would fall. She made it up to the helicopter just fine and the crew transported her to the hospital.

The crew found a hospital with a helicopter pad on the roof. They landed, but there were no lights and no one came to the roof to receive their patient. LT Smith sent down Brian, his Flight Mechanic, to see what was going on. When Brian came back he told the crew that there was no way to get the woman down to the emergency room except for them to carry her. So Chuck and Brian carried her down stairs to the ER. They quickly returned to the helicopter and went back for the others.

When they finally made it back to Air Station New Orleans, they were welcomed with a cot and some food. It wasn't the best food, nor was it a hot plate, but it would replenish their energy for tomorrow. They would have loved a shower too, but there was no water. "The accommodations weren't the greatest, but we weren't expecting much, actually we were lucky to get a cot, there were people sleeping in the halls right on the floor." Chuck had been sweating all day and swimming around in the most horrific solution of chemicals one could imagine. Not being able to shower was more than disturbing and uncomfortable it was unhealthy; a shower would have been more of decontamination than a soothing wash, but oh-well they did what they had to do. Day two things were a little different.

Chuck recalls some of the things that were not obvious to those observ-ing what was going on from their television sets. He conveyed the long arduous days he spent preparing many of the survivors for rescue. All the Rescue Swimmers assisting in New Orleans at one time or another were left on rooftops and apartment buildings for hours at a time loading people and preparing them for hoists. Many of the roofs had been torn up by the storm, so when the helicopters came into a hover, their rotor wash would blow shingles and debris all over the place. The strong wind would accelerate the particles that would many times hit and sting the swim-mers. They also had to deal with fiberglass when climbing through holes that were cut in some of the roofs to access the people that were trapped inside. None of this was forced upon Chuck or his Rescue Swimmer counterparts, these brave men and women pushed their bodies and souls to the extreme in order to help others. "My body took a beating, but in the end it was all worth it. Every single minute I spent on a rooftop and every shingle that smacked me in the back was for the greatest cause."

Then there was the sun. The exposure was brutal for everyone that had to endure it. Not knowing he was going to spend so much of his day out in direct sunlight, Chuck didn't have sunscreen with him. He got pretty burnt, but eventually the supplies starting coming in and he got a hold of some. The sun and shingles weren't the only hazards, Chuck was actually hit by a door that took flight from the rotor wash of a helicopter. Complicating some of the rescues was the fact that there were many incidences where the victims were on the lower floors. Many of them could not make it to the roof, so the swimmers would have walk down two or three flights of stairs and carry the people up to the roof. Needless to say, Chuck proved that he has what it takes and the respect of his crew.

His third day over the city, Chuck could sense the desperation in the survivors. "The people were getting a little rowdy, and they were more upset and wanted to know what was going on. "I came across several men that were very adamant in regards to their families being separated. I totally understand where they were coming from. The situation was getting pretty bad." On the third day he spent more time on rooftops and building tops and got to talk to more and more survivors. Spending time preparing them for rescue, he got a sense of what they were living through and how their lives had changed. "A lot of people asked me how this could've happened and what the plan was to rescue everybody. They wanted to know how there could be helicopters seemingly everywhere yet they had to wait three days to be picked up." Chuck explained the situation the best he could with the information he had. "We could only take it one rescue at a time."

Unfortunately, Chuck saw several people that didn't make it. Despite what he saw he tried not to let it bother him. He was more concerned with keeping focused and tried to divert the attention of the living away from the dead. He said he saw looting, "It was obvious, people were going right into gas stations and stores then coming out with stuff. There was no question what was going on." During his time Chuck even experienced a little comic relief; in fact it was comic relief for his entire crew.

On one rooftop he was lowered down to, he found four guys on their roof with a beer in hand and a cooler of beer beside them. Although somewhat comical at first, it upset Chuck because alcohol only acts to dehydrate a person when consumed and it also exacerbates an already trying situation for those in the area. "These guys were tomorrow's hospital transport waiting to happen. I wanted to do my part in preventing it." Chuck picked up the cooler and dumped it over the edge of the roof. The guys were not happy at all with his well intentioned intervention, but what were they going to do with a helicopter hovering overhead and a fully rigged rescue Swimmer telling them it was a bad idea to drink in the sun without any water.

On the fourth day, the people began swarming the helicopter when it landed. Some people cried with relief when Chuck went down to rescue them and others were upset that it had taken him so long to get there. The crew was able to fly only a few hours on their fourth day, as this was the day they were ordered to come back to Houston for some much deserved rest. Despite the feeling of wanting to stay and not abandon all the survivors that were left, Chuck knew this was the best thing. Fresh crews and helicopters were already on their way. "Our helicopter needed the maintenance and we needed the break. The fresh crews would be useful and more alert. Adrenaline can only take you so far."

On the trip back to Houston, Chuck couldn't help but think of one truly significant person he met during his time in New Orleans. He remembered that the night before, they had stopped to pick up some people from a rooftop but were unable to take them all. He had since wondered if anyone had come back to rescue them or if they made it to safety some other way. He didn't want to leave them, but the helicopters can only carry so many survivors. He recalled that during his time on the roof he spoke with an older gentleman whose questions Chuck entertained. Chuck told him everything was going to be okay and that the Coast Guard would keep coming back until "we rescue you all." Toward the end of the conversation the older gentleman asked him his name, "My friends call me Chuck." Chuck eventually left that rooftop. The older gentleman and several others survivors were left behind, but Chuck's crew had every intention of passing the word on to other crews or come back for these survivors themselves.

The morning of day four, the crew returned right back to the same apartment building roof where he had met this older gentleman. When Chuck went down to the roof the older gentleman was still there, "Chuck, Chuck... hey, you're back!" This put things in perspective for Chuck and made it all so much more personal. It made him realize that despite all the devastation that Katrina had caused and some of the bad things that a few negative people were doing, the people of New Orleans still had hope.

He, and every fellow Coastie rescuer were the hope that the hundreds and thousands of people could always count on. No accomplishment had ever felt so great. These heroes had never been a part of something so significant and so heart warming. No one could ever take this away from them.

There is nothing in Chuck's career that compares to the events of Hurricane Katrina. He knows he's still young in his career, but he can't help but feel pride and excitement knowing that he made a difference in so many people's lives. That is a joy that many people in this world will never get to experience. Driven by his dedication and honor, Chuck will continue doing good things and helping those in need. On this particular mission, he was responsible for saving 183 lives immediately after the storm. Chuck was awarded the Air Medal for his heroic actions as a United States Coast Guard Rescue Swimmer. What a way to start a career!

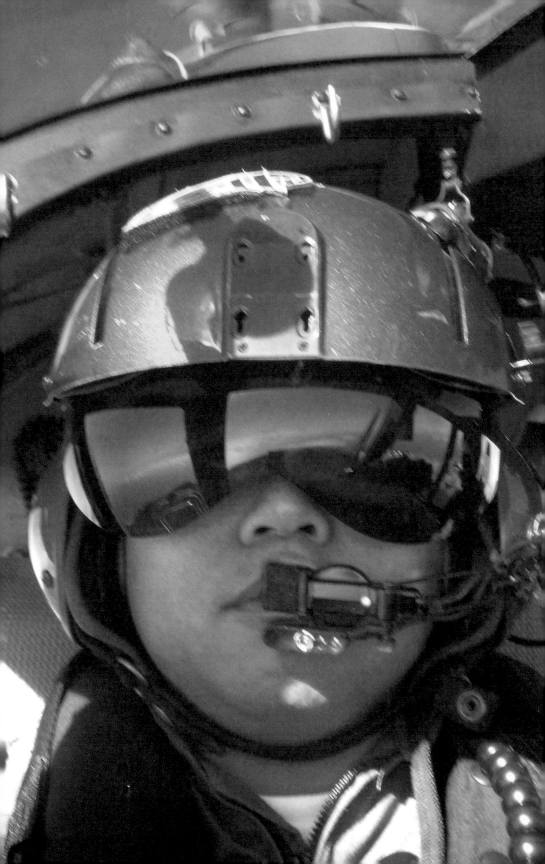

AIRCRAFT COMMANDER
Lt. Charles Guerrero

5

The son of a retired Navy Senior Chief, one would expect that LT Charles Guerrero would have traveled the world and attended many different schools in his younger years. This however was not the case for our friend "Chuck". His father was able to stay put or leave his family for short periods to complete duty obligations. The Navy stationed Chuck's father at Naval Base Charleston, which had many afloat and shore units offering him the opportunity to transfer within the same geographic location.

The youngest of three sons, Chuck was born in Charleston, SC on September 24, 1974. He was raised in Ladson, SC until the age of 18. Chuck's father was a Filipino immigrant who enlisted as a steward in the U.S. Navy's migrant program. This program allowed Filipinos to join the Navy as stewards under the Military Bases Agreement between the United States and the Republic of the Philippines of March 14, 1947. A humble steward who used to serve Navy Officers in their wardrooms, Chuck's father retired as a Senior Chief, and fulfilled his American dream that extended to his son Chuck who has now become one of the "Masters."

Family values are at the core of traditional Filipino families, and Chuck's was no exception. In fact his Aunt Helen lived with the Guerreros and adjusted her work schedule so that she could be home and act as a nanny. Mrs. Guadalupe Guerrero, also a Filipino immigrant, migrated to the U.S. under a civilian Registered Nurse recruiting program and worked the evening shift for a majority of Chuck's childhood. This type of family living is typical in their family. Filipino families are known for the importance they place on families and the caring of children. Aunt Helen's love and support combined with dedicated parents ensured someone was always home with the Guerrero boys. There was always someone teaching them right from wrong, helping them complete school work or replacing the head on that snare drum Chuck likes to call an instrument.

As Chuck grew older, his interest in a life of military service began to grow. The example set by his father had created a lasting impression of hard work and dedication for a life centered on a military career. Having a father in the Navy obviously opened Chuck's eyes to the Navy, but that all changed for him in the last month of intermediate school. In the spring of his 8th grade year was the annual Career Day Fair which turned out to be a day that would change Chuck's life forever. That day he stumbled on another "Sea-Going" service; the United States Coast Guard. He had heard about the Guard before, but he didn't really know much about the organization that seemed to base itself on rescuing people. Intrigued Chuck read about the missions, saw pictures of the small boats, cutters, airplanes and helicopters. One particular pamphlet stood out and gave him the information on how to start his adult life. The informative flyer covered the Mighty "Dauphin," the Coast Guard's HH-65 helicopter and showed a 65 hoisting a Rescue Swimmer down to a survivor at sea. From that point on he knew, "I want to be a CG Helicopter Pilot."

Although there are several routes for one to become a helicopter pilot in the U.S. Coast Guard, Chuck took one of the toughest ones. With good grades in school, military service running through his blood, and a proud Eagle Scout, Chuck made it his goal to get accepted into the U.S. Coast Guard Academy (USCGA). Known as one of the toughest and most selective colleges in the nation, he had his work cut out for him. His dedication and desire would definitely be put to the test.

Chuck's first test would be a disappointing reality, he found out he was not accepted directly into the USCG Academy. The competition was so tight for entrance to such a selective Military Service Academy that Chuck's SAT scores were not quite high enough. There was a light at the end of the tunnel for Chuck though. He qualified for a preparatory program through The Naval Academy Prep School (NAPS) in Newport, RI. Candidates that have the academic record, but need refinement of SAT scores can attend the school and compete again. Rather than give it all up, Chuck persevered, packed up his things and left for NAPS at the end of the 1992 school year.

NAPS turned out to be a blessing in disguise. The school, run by the Navy, prepares students for Navy and Coast Guard Academy life. It teaches them the military life and prepares them academically for the challenges of freshman year at the Academy. The 10 month training program challenges prospective cadets physically and mentally, while in the process indoctrinating them into the naval service and forming the base for strong character. The hardest adjustment cadets must make is to balance academics with military performance, which is why future cadets who need to strengthen their academics attend NAPS to sharpen their skills in both areas. At NAPS, Chuck strengthened his academics as expected, and he gained another benefit. He learned the military side of Academy Life, something he didn't fully realize until he graduated from prep school.

With Coast Guard rates and ranks in his knowledge base, confidence in his academic talents and a graduation certificate in his sea-bag, Chuck took some much deserved time off at home with friends and family and then headed off to the USCGA. On reporting day, he saw some scruffy, long haired guys and fashion show divas, and thought "They don't know what they're getting into." He immediately saw the benefits of spending 10 month at NAPS. While most of his future classmates were reporting to school with the grunge look and fancy suitcases, Chuck's haircut and grooming was already to military standards. He carried a sea-bag containing some uniform items, running shoes and toiletries. All the welcome letters in the world could not prepare these "Civilians" for their first day at the CG Academy.

The first day after official check-in started at 5 a.m. when "Reveille" sounded. The loud annoying horn would have freaked-out most people awaking from a deep sleep, but Chuck was expecting it. A two mile run, some calisthenics and stretching started out their day. Just six more weeks and eight semesters to go and Chuck's dream would be realized.

Graduation day at the USCGA came in May 1997. After starting out their first day with about 350 cadets, the class of 1997 graduated a little over 160 officers. That's one hell of an attrition rate if you ask anyone, it must've been worth it for those who made it. For Chuck it was one of the best days of his life, "I finally got to enter the Coast Guard Officer Corp and get one step closer towards becoming a Helicopter Pilot." He believes that the USCGA is a very difficult place to successfully complete school, "It's a great place to be from, but not such a great place to be at." That says it all.

Following graduation, Chuck headed off to the Coast Guard Cutter (CGC) Munro in Alameda, CA. He began his first tour as an Engineering Officer in Training (EOIT). An EOIT's job is to learn all the propulsion, electrical, mechanical, firefighting systems and capabilities of the 378 foot "High Endurance Cutter". He would also manage some of the enlisted maintenance personnel that worked the propulsion and auxiliary equipment. In the two years he served onboard the CGC Munro, Chuck learned every system, developed his leadership style, and became a more seasoned Coast Guard officer. He also learned the most important part of the job; he learned how to deal with being away from homeport for thirty days or more. Life on a "big white boat" is tough, but all he really remembers are the good times. During that tour he visited Alaska, Canada, Ecuador, Guatemala, Mexico, Japan, Hawaii, and Guam. Of these ports he admits his favorite was Tokyo. On that trip the cutter left California for Japan with a Dauphin Helicopter aboard. Chuck was even allowed to fly with one of the deployed pilots. It was an amazing experience for Chuck and helped keep his dream of becoming a pilot alive.

Typically, USCGA officers go to flight school after their first ship. For Chuck this did not happen. Flight school for Chuck would be delayed a few more years because of a misunderstanding. Chuck had a problem clearing his ears of pressure and he had a problem with his knee. Given these medical issues, he thought he would never pass the medical screening process. In the military, a flight physical is known as the most thorough medical examination conducted. Pilots must be in top physical and mental condition, in Chuck's case that meant he had problems.

Thinking he wasn't qualified, Chuck adjusted. Although somewhat disappointed, he had worked hard at Naval Engineering and decided he'd make that his career path. He served as an Engineer at a shore unit for the next two years under the impression he would stay an engineer for the duration of his career. He expected that his next tour would be another shore unit, and then he imagined possibly going to a ship, where he would as an Engineering Officer. But all that changed May 2000 when a close buddy called to "catch up". His buddy was Carlito Vicencio, co-author of this book and a fellow classmate who was applying for flight school.

The conversation between Chuck and his old friend began as the usual "How are you doing?" and "What have you been up to?" type of chat.

Both these guys were on their second tour in the Coast Guard following their days at the Academy. They had similar jobs supporting the Naval Engineering fleet from shore and were essentially in the same position. Catching up was great. Reminiscing about the good times they had at the Academy, England and a Spring Break trip to Puerto Rico had created a close bond between Carlito and Chuck, but 2 years on different ships and the busy Coast Guard operational tempo was enough to put some gap in even this close friendship. What was to become the next topic of conversation would change both their lives forever.

Chuck had not applied for flight school and had given up on the idea because of his bum knee and clogged up ears, but his pal had applied several times and was considering applying again. This would be the final chances for both of them to apply since the flight school selection boards do not select LTs or higher and both Chuck and Carlito were about a year away from promotion. It would be hard enough to compete for selection to flight school under normal circumstances, but now if these guys were to apply they would be competing against younger shipmates coming fresh off a boat or even Officer Candidate school. Carlito was bent on trying one more time before having to give up the dream; Chuck on the other hand hadn't even considered it.

Having knee surgery was something that is difficult to overcome in a flight physical. His buddy told him to put in for a waiver, "If your knee doesn't hurt and you can run on it, put it in writing and get a waiver". Not being able to clear his ears is something that Chuck would not be able to get a waiver for. A pilot must be able to clear his ears to relieve pressure. Chuck could clear one ear by closing his mouth, pinching his nose and blowing out, but that worked for only one ear and he couldn't understand why. On the other end of the phone he could hear Carlito cracking up in hysterical laughter. Not knowing why Carlito was laughing, Chuck asked, "What is so funny?" The response he got was, "If you can clear one ear, just keep blowing after you clear the first ear and the second one will pop too." Chuck tried to clear his ears and sure enough the first one cleared, but this time he took it one step further and kept blowing to increase the pressure. For the first time in his life, his second ear cleared. With a new found inspiration and motivation, Chuck hung up the phone and began the waiver and application process; his dream of flying helicopters for the Coast Guard had come back to life once more.

With a
waiver in
hand and an ap-
proved flight physical,
Chuck submitted his application for flight school. Now it
was just a waiting game. He knew that
some of the most talented people would be apply-
ing for this unique and highly sought after opportunity, but he remained hopeful that all the years of hard work and dedication to the Coast
Guard would pay off. A few months later all his hopes and dreams became
a reality. The flight school selection board released their results. As Chuck
read down the list he came across his name, unfortunately he didn't rec-
ognize a lot of the names on the list. Having applied two years later than
normal for a young junior officer, all the names on the least were officers
much younger and newer to the service. As he read further on down the
list he saw that his buddy Carlito had also been picked up. This was a big
deal to Chuck because getting into flight school is a great accomplishment;

but getting
to go into such
a stringent and
tumultuous training
environment is much easier
to deal with when you get to go
through it with such a close friend.

The summer of 2001 Chuck packed up his belongings and shipped them off to Pensacola, FL. He took some time off and went back to Ladson to spent time relaxing with his family and friends. July of 2001, Carlito drove down from Baltimore, MD (where he was stationed) and the two of them started the road trip of a lifetime. The culmination of that trip was driving through the gates of Naval Air Station Pensacola. The sign at the main gate read, "Welcome to the Cradle of Naval Aviation." They were about to become part of a culture with a rich background and history.

In the months of July and August, Chuck completed the Aviation Indoctrination phase of flight training. These eight weeks were full of academics, physical fitness, and tons of swimming. Although very difficult and demanding, he completed the initial training with flying colors and was ready to advance to the primary and intermediate phases of training at Naval Air Station Whiting Field located about an hour east of Pensacola.

In between the completion of Aviation Indoctrination and Primary, Chuck had a week off to relocate and take care of any last minute items prior to diving into the intense Primary and Intermediate phases of training. Once a candidate starts the upper phases they continue uninterrupted, without leave or time off. On September 11, 2001, Chuck took a trip to Mobile, AL and The Coast Guard's Aviation Training Center. Carlito and Chuck went there to gather uniform items and pick up medical records. While shopping at the CG Exchange in Mobile they saw one of the twin towers on the TVs in the electronics department of the store. They were mostly shocked and confused at first because smoke was coming out of one of the towers. They dropped their things and approached the TV. The visions coming across that tube were disturbing at best and the news announcer was saying that a plane had just flown into one of the twin towers. Several moments later, the second plane hit. Chuck had just witnessed "9-11".

Carlito and Chuck got back in their car and hurried back to NAS Whiting Field. They immediately visited the CG Liaison office to find out if their services were needed somewhere else. They weren't given any real tasks except to check on their families who both lived on the east coast. Of course all the cell phone and land lines were tied up. They couldn't contact anyone. With flight training suspended for a few days and their class check-in date for Primary pushed back two weeks, Carlito and Chuck got in the car and headed north towards South Carolina and Baltimore to make sure their families were safe. This road trip was much different than the one that had reunited these old friends. The entire trip north was gloomy, their minds were preoccupied with the tragedy that had just occurred, and one could hear a pin drop in the back seat of the car.

They finally arrived in South Carolina and Chuck's family was doing just fine. He did find out however, that his brother Richard, who was in the U.S. Navy and served as a Corpsman, was stationed on a Navy hospital ship that was on its way to New York. The next stop was Baltimore, MD; it was now late, but Carlito and Chuck shared an uneasy feeling with Baltimore being so close to New York and the Pentagon. If only they could speak with Carlito's wife (Sherrie), they wouldn't have to make such a long trip in the middle of the night; the trip from Pensacola to South Carolina had already taken its toll. After hundreds of attempts on two cell phones and a land line, they finally reached Sherrie. Everybody was fine, and they were worried about Carlito and Chuck since they were out of contact too. With their mind at ease, they decided to relax over a few beers and spend the night at Chuck's parent's house.

The following morning they headed north once more. On the trip, Chuck had heard from his dear friend Fay Miller (fellow Coastie and soon to be wife) that her Uncle Dong Lee may have been on one of the flights that flew into the Washington D.C. area. Now traveling at 100 mph versus 70, the plan was to drop off Carlito in Baltimore and head to Washington D.C. to see if he could be of any help to Fay and her family. Sherrie and the kids were doing well in Baltimore so Chuck took off and headed towards the D.C. area. Once there he met up with Fay and found out the dreadful news. Her Uncle Lee was on American Airlines flight 77, the flight that flew into the Pentagon. There were no survivors. A day or two later they attended a memorial type funeral for Fay's uncle. The following day Chuck made his way back to Baltimore to pick up Carlito. They took off the same day, hearing from Pensacola that Flight Training would commence soon. The trip down was much more solemn and quiet. Both their worlds had changed and so had the world around them. America would never be the same and neither would their roles within the U.S. Coast Guard.

The Primary phase of flight training was a killer. Not only did candidates have to learn to fly an airplane (no small task), they also had to know every little bit of information about this airplane from memory. The torque limits, how much oil it takes, what makes it fly, how many pieces of wood are located in the cockpit, etc. etc. Some of the information was useful, and some was not. But it was part of the "weeding-out" process. Naval Aviators are the best pilots in the world, if a person is going to become part of this elite fraternity, they better want it badly and they better put out. Chuck did!

Most military training programs are crunched for time and have a lot to teach. The most common approach to teaching military students more information than they have time to learn is affectionately referred to by students and teachers alike as "The Fire Hose Method". This method may not be the best way to learn information, but it's the best way to learn information fast, because the information comes so fast it is like drinking from a fire hose. The philosophy behind it is to teach the student as much as humanly possible in the smallest amount of time and those who can't learn it or can't perform to standards are kicked out or quit on their own. It creates a great deal of stress and makes life difficult and extremely challenging, but the rewards are immense. This is one of those roads not normally traveled by your everyday person; it's the road taken by those who want to give it their all to earn the coveted "Wings of Gold".

Once Chuck completed the Primary and Intermediate phases of flight training, it was time for him to move on to the Advanced phase of training which, for Chuck, would be helicopter training. The first thing he noticed about the Advanced phase was how he was treated. Instructors were nicer, students were more laid back; it appeared as if all the stressors of flight training were removed and now he was there simply to learn how to fly helicopters. Eventually he figured out it was one of those unwritten rules. He (and his classmates) had proven themselves. They dug down deep and made it through the toughest part of flight training and were now accepted tentatively into this fraternity. Instructors became part of the solution to become a better pilot rather than the enemy who watched a student's every move and penalized them for every mistake. Life was looking up for good ole Chuck.

Chuck pinned on his "Wings of Gold" on December of 2002. This was the biggest accomplishment of his life and the realization of a dream that started at that Career Day in 8th grade. He was now ready to head out to sunny Miami, FL and his first duty station, CG Air Station Miami. Chuck had never lived in Miami but was excited to go and was looking forward to flying in clear blue skies over the beautiful waters around Miami and the Caribbean. He was all set to go until something called "Needs of the Service" knocked on his door.

"Needs of the Service" is the Coast Guard's way of saying very nicely, we have to send you somewhere else and you've got no say in the matter. It's often used to fill openings that weren't planned for or to fill a need that wasn't accounted for previously. The only problem with that scenario for Chuck was his fiancée, Faye Miller. She was supposed to be transferring to his new unit with him and they had worked out a co-location strategy so they could get married. Now all the months of working on the co-location strategy had washed down the drain. They had to figure a new plan of attack as Chuck was being transferred to CG Air Station New Orleans, and they had to find a way to get Faye there. Lucky for them, Faye had been accepted into the Graduate School program so it would just be a matter of finding a good school in the New Orleans area to accept her. It finally happened, she was accepted at Tulane University.

His first day at CG Air Station New Orleans was an exciting one. Chuck couldn't believe he was actually a pilot in the Coast Guard and now he was about to set foot in a helicopter hangar and sit in the cockpit of an HH65 "Dauphin" as a pilot not a passenger. As he walked across the parking lot, he could see an air-crew stepping out of one helicopter while two parking spots down another was turning up and taxiing to the runway for takeoff. While watching that "Dauphin" takeoff and hang a sharp left towards the water, Chuck visualized his first takeoff for a SAR case. This is the excitement and job satisfaction he had been waiting for all his life; he was finally there.

Chuck's transition to CG aviation was a smooth one. As usual, the CG took care of Chuck and made him feel at home. Fellow junior officers showed him the ropes. He quickly figured out how to be successful, where to work out and who the hard-ass senior pilots were. It was all part of the life, he had proven himself in Navy Flight School and now he would have to prove himself as a co-pilot in the Coast Guard. It was all just part of the game and another day at the office for a newly minted helicopter pilot.

Within a few months, Chuck was off to his HH65 helicopter transition course. This course was always backed up, but it's the only game in town if you're a Coast Guard helicopter pilot. Compared to the Navy flight school program, the HH65 transition course is what one might consider a gentlemen's course. It's up to the student to learn the information; to learn how to fly that helicopter; to seek help if it is needed. The only requirement was; every pilot had to pass the 3 exams and the final 2 check flights. There was no one screaming or harassing anyone. Those are the positives obviously. The negatives are; everyone must motivate themselves, make time to study and keep on task.

Chuck returned to New Orleans as a qualified "Dauphin" co-pilot about 6 weeks later and jumped right into the duty schedule. Within his first month he had 2 lives saved and seen more action than he could have ever hoped for. An Air Station with 5 helicopters and two duty crews every night like Air Station New Orleans sees a lot of action and it was known for the treacherous weather and the high number of SAR cases it responded to. This was perfect for Chuck who lived for this stuff and couldn't get enough. He can still vividly recall his first life saved. "The guy we launched on was in the water between 12 to 15 hours. His boat must have capsized in the rough waters and drifted out into the Gulf. When we spotted him he was holding on to a board the size of a small door floating out in the Gulf of Mexico, in the middle of the night. He's lucky we found him. I was very happy to find him; this is what I signed up to do!"

Life as a brand new co-pilot wasn't all fun and games though. The SAR cases and the flying are actually the reward for a job well done. As an aviator and officer, flying is considered your primary job on paper. Every good aviator knows however, the way to make it in the Coast Guard is to do a good job with your desk work. All Coast Guard aviators have collateral jobs along with being a professional pilot. Some run the Engineering Department, others are "paper pushers", and some even do things like make sure the wardroom (where the officers hang out) is stocked with food and drinks. Chuck had collaterals as the Medical Officer initially then the Personnel Officer.

Eventually Chuck would upgrade to First Pilot (FP) and then to Aircraft Commander (AC), gaining valuable flight time and experience along the way. Every AC has to meet the same standards and possess the same basic skill sets, but there is a big difference between a brand new AC and the veteran who's seen it all. Chuck was now a new AC responsible for the safety of his crew, the $10 Million helicopter and the lives of those he setout to rescue. It was a huge lift, but that is his job. That is why he gets paid the big bucks.

The first big hurricane to threaten New Orleans while Chuck was stationed there was Hurricane Ivan. Hurricane Ivan was the strongest hurricane of the 2004 season and eventually struck near Gulf Shores, Alabama. As Ivan approached aircrews and aircraft evacuated from Air Station New Orleans and ATC Mobile Alabama. All those crews ran to Texas and Air

Station Houston. Chuck was a member of one of the New Orleans crews. At one point there were twelve helicopters on the ramp in Houston. Of course those that had a friend in Houston stayed with them, and Carlito just happened to be stationed there, so Chuck and his wife hung out with their old friends Carlito and Sherrie. When he was directed to return to assess the damage and aid in the rescue effort, Chuck left his wife in the care of the Vicencio family and returned to the devastated area to lend assistance. The damage caused by Ivan, although costly, did not require the kind of rescue effort Chuck was about to live through with Hurricane Katrina. He spent the next couple of days flying over the damaged areas, dropping off supplies, and providing logistics flights.

In the spring of 2005, Chuck's wife Faye (Guerrero) was nearly completed with her MBA from Tulane University and received orders to her new duty station in Honolulu, HI. Chuck on the other hand still had one year left to serve in New Orleans, but was able to negotiate a mid-season transfer that would separate the two LTs for about 6 months or so. The CG needed Chuck to send his wife out to Hawaii alone and he would meet her there in 6 months. Not having any children at the time made the situation easier to handle. Faye moved to Hawaii, and Chuck put their home on the market in hopes of selling it prior to his transfer at the end of the 2005 calendar year.

Chuck received several offers on his house, and finally accepted one of the more reasonable offers. The agents got the ball rolling on the paperwork late July/ early August '05, and then Hurricane Katrina came into the picture. Everyday he grew more and more concerned, well aware that house closings don't normally continue if there is a hurricane in the Gulf of Mexico. Fortunately for him, Hurricane Katrina was still in Florida and hadn't entered the Gulf. Closing continued and he was able to sell his house.

Hurricane Katrina eventually headed into the Gulf of Mexico with her sights on the coast of Louisiana and Mississippi. Back at CG Air Station New Orleans, Chuck along with his fellow shipmates were making preparations should they have to evacuate. As the Personnel Officer Chuck had to prepare hurricane recall rosters, evacuation instructions and safeguard all personnel records. It was very important that he complete the recall rosters way in advance. Knowing where people planned on evacuating and publishing the names of the fly-away crews was critical to the success of the follow-on recovery efforts and to the safety of the personnel and their families. Securing personnel records was a huge endeavor. Although a lot of paperwork is now kept electronically, personnel records contained personal and career information of the crew that the station could not afford to lose.

As Hurricane Katrina drew near, concern throughout the Air Station was evident. Crew members were boarding up their own houses, packing up irreplaceable valuables and sending off their families. Having relocated to an apartment and storing other items in a commercial storage unit because of his upcoming move, Chuck preceded to help out his shipmates. The two days prior to Hurricane Katrina's impact, Chuck spent his time on the final preparations at work as well as assisting others in preparing their homes and families for what was about to become a reality. The day prior to Hurricane Katrina making land fall, Chuck evacuated to Houston to wait out the storm. He had been chosen as a member of a helicopter fly-away crew this time around, and Chuck's responsibility to his unit was to get out of the impact zone safely and await further instruction for his return. He evacuated for the second time in two back to back hurricane seasons to the Vicencio family's home in Houston, TX. His wife Faye evacuated several hours later and ran into significantly more traffic, eventually making a safe arrival to the Houston area.

The morning of August 29, 2005 Carlito and Chuck woke up first thing in the morning and headed to CG Air Station Houston to get the latest scoop on plans for a rescue effort and to catch up on the latest reports of damage in the impact zone. Carlito was put on a crew that would depart on day three. Chuck was instructed to be ready to go back as soon as they had a helicopter available for him. After waiting several days without a helicopter he could fly back, Chuck took a ferry flight with an Air Station Houston crew and eagerly returned to the devastated New Orleans area.

The flight back to New Orleans was an eye opener to say the least. Trees for miles and miles in the western Louisiana area had lain down before the winds of Hurricane Katrina. Small ditches were now rivers overflowing into roadways. Entering Louisiana, Chuck could see that power was definitely out in the area and that significant damage had occurred. There was however not too much flooding in the area, just a lot of debris, downed power lines and significant structural damage to buildings and homes. Immediately upon his return to Air Station New Orleans, Chuck checked on the personnel records he had secured along with the unit's recall rosters and found that they had all survived the hurricane. His next step was to head over to Maintenance Control, where they were issuing helicopters for ready crews to head out into the disaster zone. Chuck took the first helicopter available to him, grabbed a co-pilot, flight mechanic and rescue swimmer and launched to aid in the rescue efforts.

Nearing sunset, it was clearly evident that there was no electricity in New Orleans. Chuck's initial goal was to survey the area and see where his services could be the most beneficial. What he encountered was shocking; there were thousands of people still in the area. For some reason, the city of New Orleans had not evacuated completely as he had expected. Immediately he reacquainted himself and his crew with the flight safety hazards in the area, and they began their rescue operations. His first rescue would be a trying one.

While surveying the area for hazards, a crewmember spotted a family and their dog on top of their roof signaling for help. Chuck circled back around after flying over them once then began his rescue checklist to bring the helicopter into position to affect a rescue. The first hoist went well, pulling a lady off the rooftop into safety. The second hoist was a little more complicated due to the limitations of the "Dauphin" Bravo model aircraft. It is a well known fact that the engines on the "Dauphin" helicopter are severely underpowered. Constant monitor and finessing of the aircraft controls were crucial to ensuring that he didn't burn-up an engine. As they dropped back into position to hoist the lady's husband, they completed their rescue checklist once more and sent the hoist and rescue basket down to the rooftop. To their surprise, the man put his dog into the basket and then followed the animal in.

This is an issue that all CG crews that would fly in this rescue effort would encounter. Although the CG crews were not there to rescue pets, people were understandably unwilling to leave them behind. While Chuck held the helicopter in a steady, stable hover, the flight mechanic brought the hoist up. This immediately took its toll on the limited engines. As the man and his dog were brought into the helicopter cabin, the safety pilot called out "MGT, MGT.". This meant that the instrumentation gauges were showing excessive temperatures in the Engines. Chuck had to make a split second decision. His choices were to either burn up the engine a little bit and let the maintenance crew at the Air Station inspect the engine or risk settling his helicopter, crew and survivors into the big trees that were lurking a few feet below. Chuck pulled in power cautiously and flew out of harms way. They delivered the couple and their dog to safety and returned back to base for fuel and a new aircraft.

The next sortie would raise a few more hairs on the backs of their necks. It was now sunset and the power grids were out in the entire area. Chuck knew flying at night with that much helicopter traffic, no city lights and lack of air traffic control would test his limits. As an Aircraft Commander he had to think about the safety of his crew. He knew they were headed into uncharted territories and that the mission was much more dangerous than anything he or his aircrew had ever experienced. In the final moments before takeoff, Chuck asked his crew "How's everyone doing, are you all cool with what we are doing?" After he got the nod from his crew that everyone was comfortable with the mission at hand, Chuck and his crew took off into the devastated areas in search of more survivors.

Flying the area that night was different than the typical night flights Chuck was used to in the New Orleans. The first thing that stood out was the vast darkness that existed in place of the New Orleans' lighted skyline. As he thought about what had happened to this great town, his Flight Mechanic called out flashing lights in an apartment complex. Suddenly it was apparent that many of the survivors who had remained indoors during the incredible daytime heat were now signaling for help with lighters, flashlights and other various lights. This apartment complex was not the only one full of people signaling for help. Talking to his buddies over the radio, Chuck quickly realized that other aircrews were encountering the same situation. The aircrew completed their Rescue Checklists and proceeded to a hover over the apartment complex.

They hoisted survivors from balconies, rooftops, stairs, and water-filled parking lots. Chuck and his crew continued to operate this way for the next 5 hours, saving over 30 people that night. With the lack of visual references, lights or a visible horizon, this was one of the most challenging hovering Chuck had ever done. "It made me a better pilot, there was no time to be tired or make excuses. I kept the aircraft in position and my flight mechanic and rescue swimmer went to work. The rush and adrenaline kept us going. Time flew by, we didn't want to stop flying, but we had reached our maximum flight hours as a crew." Chuck returned to the Air

Station that night maxed-out on flight time. Letting all the visual images and that night's missions sink in, he fell asleep at his desk only to awake 5 hours later and get ready to do it all over again.

The following days presented even more unique missions for his aircrew. By this time the Army and Navy helicopters had showed up and Air Traffic was even more crowded. The danger this presented was that the Army and Navy talk to each other on different radio frequencies than the Coasties did. What they basically had was three different military helicopters talking on different radio channels and not talking to each other. This caused some confusion, but everyone pressed on and thankfully there were no collisions during these rescue operations.

The congestion in the air forced Chuck to open up his comfort zone and at the same time fly with extra caution. It was not uncommon to be conducting a rescue in a hover 30 feet from another rescue helicopter, with a news chopper directly in front filming while several other helicopters circled above waiting to come in for some rescues themselves. On one occasion, Chuck and his aircrew were in a hover in between power lines and trees hoisting a mom and her child from a trapped parking lot; while in the house directly in front there was another helicopter performing a similar hoist 10 yards ahead and only 30 feet higher. Unsure if the other helicopter was aware of his helicopter, Chuck had to maintain his hover position and wait for that helicopter to take off. If he had taken off before the other one he could have interrupted that rescue or flown through the other helicopter's rotor wash, which is not good from an aerodynamic standpoint. It was a lot of information to manage and too many decisions to make in a matter of seconds, but all the Naval Flight School and Coast Guard training had paid off. Chuck was a well trained machine, prepared and ready for everything and anything that came his way.

Since the Pontchartrain levees had failed and literally filled up part of the city with water from the lake, people had been trapped, prisoners of the deluge. It was the old, young and invalid who were affected the most. Chuck and his crew performed a rescue that he considered, "…That rescue was the reason I was in New Orleans at that time…" The rescue occurred in the Uptown area of New Orleans. What made the situation a little more difficult was that power lines were down everywhere, gas lines were bubbling in the water, and the houses were about 4 feet apart with tall trees all around them. Assessing the area, Chuck spotted a man hanging out of his second story window waving a white towel at the helicopter.

The crew completed all rescue checklists and Chuck brought the helicopter into a steady hover position. The flight mechanic then sent the rescue swimmer down on the hoist cable to affect the rescue. The swimmer climbed in the window to talk with the man to see if there were additional survivors. He radioed back to the helicopter with the information that there were three males in the apartment and that they were refusing to come up. He said they would prefer that the crew go to the house next door first. He reported that there was a couple next door that needed the assistance more urgently and that the female was in a wheel chair as she could not walk.

Immediately, Chuck picked up his swimmer and positioned the helicopter at the neighboring house. They completed their checks and hoisted the swimmer down. Once down on-scene the swimmer realized this was going to be a tough rescue. The woman could not walk at all and was somewhat delusional from the heat and stress. He managed to maneuver her and rig her for pickup, and then he gave the flight mechanic the "thumbs up" for pickup. The next rescue was also a little complicated. The next person was a man who had only one arm, but the rig used for rescue tucks under both arms. Not wanting to waste anymore time, the swimmer hooked-up first, then strapped the man to him and requested pickup. From the aircraft, the crew waved to the three guys who selflessly gave up a flight to safety. The crew signaled to them that they'd be right back. Chuck dropped off the couple at a nearby landing zone, one that was accepting ambulatory survivors, then went right back to the scene.

Back on scene, Chuck completed 3 quick hoists and pulled those guys out of the house. On the trip to a nearby airport that was transporting survivors to safety via buses, the men shared that their father had passed away and was floating in-between the two houses they just left. It was amazing that despite the tragedy of losing their father, these men were still able to remain positive and would give up their own initial rescue to save their neighbors who were in more need of assistance. The couple they had reported to Chuck was inside and had all but given up. They weren't signaling for help or trying to get out of their house. "Had it not been for these guys, that couple probably wouldn't have made it."

The following days, Chuck didn't get to fly much as other Coast Guard Air Stations had sent pilots to give all these guys rest. He did take the occasional flight, to get out of the office, and one such flight tested his levels of comfort. This situation came about when his crew spotted over 200 people on a rooftop. These people had been indoors waiting things out to see if power or water would come back. By then they had given up and were on a big building rooftop signaling for help and of course they all wanted to be the first to leave the rooftop. Since the rooftop was big and still appeared steady and stable, Chuck landed the helicopter on the flat roof so the survivors could climb in rather than having to hoist them one by one. Immediately upon landing, a mob of people swarmed his helicopter and were trying to climb in one way or another. His flight mechanic and rescue swimmer jumped out and forcibly moved the crowd back away from the helicopter and explained the proper protocols for receiving rescue. They loaded up the first 5 and took off to a nearby landing zone. Seeing that they could not rescue all these people themselves, Chuck called for assistance from the Coast Guard HH-60J "Jayhawk" helicopters in the area that had larger cabins and equipped with the power to carry larger loads of people. Three showed up on scene and within an hour or two had rescued the remaining survivors.

The Hurricane Katrina experience was humbling, exciting and a sad time all rolled into one event. It was humbling to see the devastation that one storm could cause in one town, exciting to be able to test your flying skills and save so many people and sad because a great tragedy had just occurred and so many people lost so much. Chuck was glad he could help and loved the fact that he could be a part of this historic rescue effort. He's proud of his fellow Coasties and proud of his Coast Guard. Chuck was awarded a United States Air Medal for his heroic service during the Hurricane Katrina rescue efforts where he worked day and night for weeks and saved 94 lives. During Hurricane Rita, which followed a month later in the eastern Texas, Chuck earned his second "Air Medal"; oddly enough on his birthday.

RESCUE SWIMMER
AST3 David McClure

6

It takes a special type of person to become a Coast Guard Rescue Swimmer.
They are unique in this world because
of the nature of the risks they accept the
moment they step out of their helicopter. The fact that there aren't many
Rescue Swimmers in the world makes them as unique as being a racecar
driver or a professional athlete, but we're not necessarily talking about the
same thing. A Rescue Swimmer is a well-oiled machine who is an expert
in many fields. He is a paramedic, a professional class swimmer, and your
best friend in time of need, all wrapped into one. Unique may be an un-
derstatement when you take into account all the talents that get fused into
this one person. The general public never really gets a good look into the
lives of one of these special individuals unless they happen to be a friend
or family member, or possibly had their lives saved by one of these men or
women.

Many high performing men and women in the Coast Guard have taken
on the challenge of trying to become a Rescue Swimmer. The acceptance
rate however is very low and the attrition rate is greater than fifty percent.
What that means is that the applicants that are lucky enough to get a shot
at going to Rescue Swimmer School have less than a fifty percent chance
to make it through the program. That can be a disappointment and dis-
couraging to people who make the decision to attempt this great feat. It's
not like getting a four-year college degree or attending a two-year program
somewhere. In those programs, if you set your mind to it, you stand a
great chance at making it through. In the Rescue Swimmer program, you
can want it all you want, but if you don't have what it takes you will not
make it, no matter how hard you try.

AST3 David McClure, born in 1982 to Regina and David McClure, didn't
quite know what he wanted to do with his life in his younger years. A

quiet man from Jacksonville, FL, Dave comes from a humble background that may sound similar to many American families. His light hair and slight surfer attitude present a casual demeanor that shows semblance of the Florida beaches he carries in his soul.

Dave lived through a typical childhood until about the age of ten. At that time in his life he lived in Yulee, FL, and his parents decided to split up. Dave moved back to Jacksonville, FL with his mother and had to start all over again in a brand new elementary school. Speaking with Dave it appears he was a flexible and well adjusted young man even at the age of 10. He spoke of the divorce and having to fit in and make new friends in school as if it were no big deal at all. Dave just said, "It's part of life and kind of made me who I am today." His mother eventually remarried and Dave lived with his Mom and Stepfather in Jacksonville, FL until he enlisted in the Coast Guard.

Dave's high school years were again, somewhat normal, although they were probably a little crazier and included more partying than most. He liked to party, and his mother let him go about his business without being too judgmental. In fact, his story regarding how he found out about the Coast Guard involves some jail time, which Dave served during his younger years. He didn't get into the details however, he linked that time in his life and that specific event to him deciding to join the military. We're assuming Dave needed a little discipline in his life, and the military is just the place to get some of that. Whatever it was that he did however, bear in mind that it couldn't have been too bad because the Coast Guard will not allow someone in the service that has a criminal record. He did share with us that sitting in a jail cell made him realize that he had some growing up to do and since he didn't see college in his near future, he decided to join the military until he figured out what he wanted to do with his life.

Initially Dave decided he would join the U.S. Air Force. He had met with the recruiter, filled out all the necessary paperwork and was ready to "Aim High", until a conversation with a neighbor's U.S. Navy friend changed all that. His new acquaintance told him all about the U.S. Coast Guard, a service Dave knew nothing about at the time. All this talk of the Coast Guard didn't convince him right away, but it struck his curiosity enough that it led him to find a local recruiting office and see what the Coast Guard was all about.

From the time he decided to join the Air Force, recruiters from all the other branches had been calling Dave as well. They all wanted to change his mind and would give him the typical 5-minute recruiting speech that they used to present their service as the organization of choice. With all the overbearing sales pitches he had to endure, Dave was happy to meet the Coast Guard recruiter. "This guy was so relaxed and had a laid back attitude, almost like he didn't care if I joined or not. I remember him telling me that I could join if I wanted to and that he'd get the paperwork if I wanted, but he wasn't pushy and he didn't have me sign papers." Maybe that was his attitude or he could sense that Dave was sick and tired of the overbearing sales pitches, but it was his demeanor and attitude that got Dave hooked in the end. This was the kind of military Dave was looking for, one with cool jobs but nice people as well. At first glance, the Coast Guard had the allure of the ocean, ships, helicopters and boarding officers with guns, but Dave was looking for something more, and that recruiter made a lasting impression on him that would change his life forever.

After getting through the initial interview and big picture questions with the recruiter, they got into specifics. One of the aspects of the Coast Guard that Dave appreciated the most was that he didn't have to pick his career right away. He found out that in the Coast Guard, people go through boot camp and then straight to a duty station. They don't go through any specialized training in a career field they are forced to commit to before they ever know anything about the service. Dave had the opportunity to join the Coast Guard and serve for a while before having to decide on what he wanted to do for the rest of his life.

The first step in the enlistment process was taking the Armed Services Vocational Aptitude Battery (ASVAB). This test is used to sort out the candidate pool and places them in categories of jobs they qualify for based on their test scores. Basically, the higher the score, the more jobs a candidate can qualify for. People with lower scores are more limited in what the military will train them to do. The second step is the medical physical. They get a complete checkup, from eyes to ears, to elbows and feet; not one thing gets by these doctors. The goal here is the make sure the candidate pool have sound bodies and minds that are ready, fit and able to perform the strenuous duties that the military requires. They even toss in a drug test to make sure candidates are in compliance with our zero tolerance drug use policy even before they enter the service. If all goes well

with these initial screening processes, the candidate is sworn into military service and is given a date to report to Boot Camp.

Boot Camp is where the military takes over your life. This is where Dave realized that they owned him for as long as he wanted to be a part of the team. During Boot Camp he was told when to run, eat, sleep, study, and shower. Even what kind of haircut he would sport or what kind of clothes he would wear were decisions that were not left up to Dave. Every minute of every day was accounted for. His only free time was in his dreams, and even they were probably monitored. For Dave, the first few days seemed like "...the biggest mistake of my life. I thought, what the hell am I doing here, I must have been crazy. These guys aren't as cool as my recruiter was."

Like many recruits, conforming to life as a "maggot" was not appealing or pleasant. Being yelled at in the face by a Drill Instructor who seems to have eyes in the back of his head and who doesn't forget anything wrong you did was enough to break many recruits down. Dave witnessed many of these instances and saw a lot of good people drop out. The theory is however that serving in the military is the most stressful occupation anyone can choose. These young men and women will get a lot of responsibility very early in their lives and many of them will have to make tough decisions in the heat of battle. If they can't handle the stress, military organizations such as the Coast Guard would rather pass on their services and offer them a plane ticket home. The ones that make it through however get sent to their first duty station to serve as the "non-rates" while they figure out what they want to be when they grow up. In the mean time they perform all the menial tasks and do all the work no one else wants to do.

When the events of September 11, 2001 occurred Dave was in Boot Camp. He did not get to witness the live feeds because in Boot Camp he was not allowed to watch TV. The following day however, his instructors pulled a TV into the classroom, which shocked all the recruits. The video they were about to see was going to be an even bigger shocker. The instructors played the video of the planes crashing into the towers and parts of a news cast. Rumors had been going around, but they were all unconfirmed for Dave until he saw the video. They could not believe their eyes. They all stared at the video in awe as this horrible event unfolded. They were then briefed on the situation and told of the Muslim extremists that executed these suicide missions in order to kill innocent Americans by flying airplanes into the World Trade Center buildings. Despite the trauma, Dave pressed on and continued to work hard toward graduation. On his graduation day, based on his class ranking, he selected an open position at Coast Guard Group Mobile, AL as an E-2 Seaman Apprentice.

In his first six months at Group Mobile, Dave was assigned to the cleanup crew for the entire facility. Basically he was paying his dues as a janitor for a little while as the low man on the totem pole. It was okay though, Dave was aware that these less savory and uninspiring tasks go to the junior guys. Soon enough he would earn the right not to have to do them anymore and after a pretty quick six months he was reassigned to the Group Aids to Navigation Branch (ATON). This job was more challenging and included a little more responsibility. Dave's main duties included moving buoys around, cleaning them, performing preventative maintenance and inspecting them for service at sea. He was performing a very important job that greatly helps mariners. ATON is one of the Coast Guard's most important jobs that actually goes unnoticed because it's not exciting. Since 1939 however, when congress moved the Lighthouse Service under the Coast Guard's umbrella of responsibility, the Coast Guard has been performing this service for the mariners of American waters. Prior to 1939, the Lighthouse Administration bounced around several different government agencies and did not get its due attention.

Dave worked in Group Mobile's ATON branch for the next year and a half. He actually enjoyed his time there because it was a small work crew that kept busy and he didn't have to deal with the more senior people or all the office politics that some of his other buddies were going through. In his time there, Dave passed the required exams and kept out of trouble and moved up in rank from E-2 (Seaman Apprentice) to E-3 (Seaman). Once he made the rank of Seaman (SN), he finally made his decision on what rate he wanted to pursue. After much investigation, Dave discovered he had a passion for Search and Rescue and in particular the Rescue Swimmer's role.

There were no guarantees that he would be accepted. The application process for Aviation Survival Technician (AST) School is long, competitive and requires a complete medical physical to ensure that candidates are fit for flight duties. Dave completed his flight physical and filled out the necessary paperwork to have his name placed on the AST "A" School waiting list. All he could do at this point was wait until it was his turn.

Once accepted into the program, Dave was transferred to Coast Guard Air Station Mobile. Conveniently located on the same base as Group Mobile, Dave would spend some time there learning what it is to be in the aviation community. He would learn how to handle aircraft, and as is the case of soon to be ASTs, he would spend a majority of his days working out and exercising a lot. Unlike many other CG rates, ASTs are required to work-out, swim, run, etc, as part of their workday. These guys are almost like paid athletes except the pay is a lot slimmer and the risks are much higher. As you can imagine, much of Dave's time at Air Station Mobile was spent getting as ready as humanly possible for the physical demands of AST "A" School. The CG will not send an individual to AST "A" School without having some degree of confidence that this person possesses the physical fitness required to meet the grueling stresses of the school and the job. Dave would someday test that theory.

AST "A" School is extremely grueling and challenging. Even those in peak physical condition sometimes fail. Somewhere in his training, Dave missed something and didn't make it through school the first time around. Although he is not the best swimmer or runner, he could keep up with his class for the most part. He didn't get into any major trouble and only fell out of a few runs, but he found himself being sent home on his first attempt. When asked about the experience, as usual Dave shrugged it off and said, "I think I have a record for the longest time spent in Swimmer School."

After a little further discussion Dave explained that if he had to put his finger on one particular incident that forced the instructors to fail him, it would be the event where he almost drowned in the pool. This scenario was a very challenging one too! It all started with Dave and four instructors hopping in the pool. The goal of the instructors was to try to drown him. Dave's goal was to take control of the situation and each one of his instructors and affect their rescue. The instructors in turn would do whatever they could to simulate panicked victims who would drown their rescuer just to catch a breath of air. During this event Dave was pushed beneath the water several times and one time when he tried to resurface to catch his breath, he forgot to clear his snorkel and breathed in water instead of air. As he tells the story, "my lungs filled with water and I began to pass out. I saw the darkness closing in as one of the instructors pulled me to the side of the pool."

Despite this incident, Dave was allowed to continue with his training. In fact, it wasn't until he had almost completed training that he was told that he would not be graduating with his class. This was a terrible blow to anyone who had suffered through the agony and endured the pains and struggles of this training, but Dave dealt with it well and went back to his old unit. When he arrived back at Mobile, Dave was given two options. First he could choose another rate and put his name on a different "A" School list or he could try AST "A" School one more time. This brought a smile to his face. Dave had thought his dreams of becoming a Rescue Swimmer were over. Never in his wildest dreams did he think he would get a second shot at this. This time he was more ready than ever. He had been through the worst and knew what to expect of the training. All he had to do was tough it out and be a little smarter this time around. His mindset was perfect, Dave left for school confident and determined, as every future Rescue Swimmer should be.

The second time around, AST "A" School was no problem for Dave. It's not that he didn't face challenges or that he didn't struggle, it's that his mindset was different. He was harder to discourage and he knew what to expect. Additionally, Dave was in even better shape this time, having already gone through the physical training once before and mentally knowing he could do it.

The only thing he said was a little tough was one of the team events called the litter carry. A litter is similar to a gurney but without the wheels. It is the device used by Rescue Swimmers to lift a victim who is injured and cannot walk or needs to be immobilized to prevent further injury. The reason this event was so tough was because his team had to go on a two mile run with one of their team members strapped in the litter at all times.

They ran with this litter down a frozen river and then had to swim more than a mile in icy water to cross over to the other side of the beach. Once on the other side, they had to stand up their shelter and establish a camp.

As Dave tells it, "It was tough because we could see the instructor's camp with the big fire and steaks cooking on the grill, while we were still struggling to erect camp and had a tiny fire going. To top things off, it was freezing cold!" Everyone made it through this event though and the class moved on. Dave finally graduated and received orders for Coast Guard Air Station Houston, the place where he would soon make his mark on history.

A single and soft-spoken young man, Dave arrived in Houston in March 2005 and commenced the check-in process. He processed in, found a place to live, met all the important people at his new unit and commenced his training. AST "A" School was just the beginning, he still had to qualify at his new unit as a Rescue Swimmer. Without completing the Rescue Swimmer syllabus he was just a graduate from school, not a Rescue Swimmer. One of the requirements was to attend Emergency Medical Technician (EMT) School. This would take him out of town again, so his reunion with the other half of his heart would have to wait a little while longer. Something that wasn't mentioned earlier was that when Dave left for "A" school, he left someone behind in Mobile. While Dave was in EMT School, his fiancée Susan stayed with her parents in Mobile. They reunited and married in April 2005 and moved into a little apartment in Houston to start their lives together. They immediately began looking for a home to buy, and eventually found one that met their needs and was within their budget. In fact, they were supposed to close on the house during the Hurricane Katrina Relief Operations, but Dave was out of town saving lives in New Orleans.

The day prior to Hurricane Katrina, August 28, 2005, Dave was the Rescue Swimmer on duty. He was back at Air Station Houston waiting for the next SAR case. He could feel things were getting tense and that the following day would be a busy and hectic time. Hurricane Katrina made landfall early on the morning of Monday August 29th. Because of the duty schedule and the crew rest requirements Dave knew he could not go on the first wave of helicopters in support of the Rescue Efforts. He ran to the Rescue Swimmer shop and saw there was nobody there. It turns out the guys from the shop were told to come in later that day to support all the work that needed to be done to prepare the helicopters going to New Orleans.

From the get go, Dave wanted to be part of the action. Recently qualified as a Rescue Swimmer, he wanted to get experience and wanted to go do what he was trained to do. One way or another, Dave was going to get on one of those helicopters headed east. Day one and two passed by and still he hadn't received word to pack his things and get on a helicopter to New Orleans. On the third day, Wednesday, he got a phone call telling him that Rescue Swimmers from Coast Guard Air Station Miami were on their way to Houston to supplement the wave of Rescue Swimmers going to New

Orleans. Fearing that he might be left out of the action, Dave packed his things and went back to the Air Station. His strategy worked, and being the only Rescue Swimmer ready to go at the time, he got his chance and headed east with a Houston crew.

The original plan was for the crew to stay in New Orleans for a week. Once they got there however, Dave could tell that things were bad. He felt certain that with all the work that had to be done, and the living conditions they would face, that the higher ups would be prompted to supplement with fresher crews sooner than a week's time. The trip over was troubling. The damage to the area was tremendous. Dave wasn't sure just how bad it was, he just knew the visual images looked terrible.

When they finally arrived at Air Station New Orleans, they were met with some familiar faces from Houston. These crews had been there for a few days already and he could tell by their appearance they had been beat up pretty good. Their buddies quickly passed off as much information as possible and provided a lot of insight that would benefit Dave and the rest of his crew in the days ahead. After the quick "gouge" session, they got a more formal Standard Area and Situational Briefing before being set free to participate in the Rescue Efforts that were already underway. By this time the weather had gotten considerably better and helicopters from the Navy, Marines and the Army filled the ramp area along with the Coast Guard aircraft. It was definitely an impressive sight for Dave, "I couldn't believe all the different aircraft I saw as I brought my gear over to my heli-copter. It was nice to see that we could count on other services to support a mission as grand as this one. The parking lot was definitely full!"

Once their helicopter was refueled they got airborne. The first rescues Dave remembers occurred on Interstate 10. "There was a group of people near the road, several others stranded in chest deep water and a few more floating in a little boat nearby." His pilot had Dave hoisted down to assess the situation. Dave found everything to be all right, except for the fact that the people wanted to bring their bags with them and they actually asked if they could bring the boat. "We obviously could only let them bring a few things and the boat was definitely out of the question. I rigged them up one at a time and we hoisted them up. We ended up hoisting six people and then dropped them off at one of the landing zones." Little did he know - this was just the beginning.

"Helicopters were in the sky everywhere, there was no organization. I had never seen that many helicopters in the air at one time and I especially had never seen one come so close to my own. I felt a bit uncomfortable throughout because we were hovering literally a few feet from each other as we were conducting rescue operations. Things never felt unsafe, it was just a little uncomfortable. I don't see how it could've been done any differently though. I have to give it to my Pilots, they did an outstanding job keeping us from running into another helicopter." The experience appeared to have impacted Dave somewhat, but he always trusted his Pilots. Traffic avoidance is always a danger in a large aviation effort such as this one. Good communications between aircraft is the key to avoiding mid-air collisions, and although communications weren't ideal and not everyone was talking on the same frequency, there was enough communication, and the pilots were all skilled enough to overcome this huge hurdle and complete the operation with no collisions.

One case that stuck with Dave was the rescue of a woman who had actually evacuated the area before Hurricane Katrina struck New Orleans. Dave was left on scene with her for some time while he prepared another more critical survivor for hoisting. He had the opportunity to chat with her for a little before rescuing her as well and found out that she came back after the hurricane passed to pick up a few more things that she would need to help her get by. While she was packing up her things and listening to the radio, she heard that the Pontchartrain levees were breaking and that the area her home was in would soon be flooded. She packed as quickly as she could, but within 20 minutes of hearing that broadcast, the car and the first story of her house were flooded. "It was shocking to me how quickly all the flooding happened." Dave sent her up and then transported her to safety leaving the irony of this entire situation behind in the floods.

A big problem that Dave encountered throughout his rescues was the size of some of the victims. He shared with us that many of them didn't fit through windows, required large holes to be cut in the roofs, and some didn't even fit in the rescue basket. On one case that ran late into the evening, Dave told of a woman who was in dire need of assistance. He wouldn't guess what her weight was, but he did say that she did not fit in the rescue basket. The only other way to get her up to the helicopter was to use a technique called the Double-Lift Method. This required the use of two strops to rig the survivor and then the Rescue Swimmer and survivor get hoisted up to the helicopter at the same time. Bear in mind that the hoist is only rated for 600 lbs, "We came real close to exceeding the limits on that hoist. I could hear the hoist whining and screeching and the helicopter was moving as we swung a little underneath the rotor-wash." According to the pilots, they were real close to exceeding engine limits on the helicopter and they experienced so much movement that they thought something might have gone wrong in the back. That's part of being a Rescue Swimmer though. They need to be able to overcome and adapt to every situation. Not every situation is the same and not every survivor fits the typical survivor mold that they're used to from training.

On a similar case or at least similar circumstances, Dave found himself in an apartment building with three larger women that definitely were not going to fit through the window where he entered. Not only was the window somewhat small, but also swinging these women would put a great burden on the hoist due to the momentum of the swinging motion. Having to find a secondary way out, he asked the women if the apartment door was open to which they replied that it was. Dave called his Pilots on his radio and asked to be hoisted up so he could explain the situation further. Once back in the cabin, he explained the situation and was hoisted to the porch this time to try and gain access to the survivors via the front door.

As luck would have it, the door was locked. Thinking back to the many movies and TV shows he had seen recently, Dave thought he could just kick the door in without a problem. That would not be the case. Dave would kick it with his foot and ram it with his shoulder over 20 times before he was able to break through. "After kicking it that hard over 20 times, I was ready to give up, but I gave one last shot and this time I was able to break it down." He went upstairs to get the survivors and carried the oldest one over his shoulder. It was an exhausting rescue after having to break the door down and carry a survivor over his shoulder, but it was all worth it once he saw their happy faces inside his helicopter.

A great example of unique situations and rescues is the story of an elderly woman Dave rescued. His pilots hoisted him down to a three-story house where they saw an old lady waving for help. When he got down there he was informed that the lady's husband was down stairs and that she refused to leave without him. Dave communicated his intentions of going down and looking for the man to his Pilots, knowing that they were low on fuel.

He got the okay, but was told to hurry it up as they only had a few minutes of fuel left before having to depart the scene. Dave quickly went down the stairs and searched for a few minutes with no luck. At this point the thought ran through his mind that maybe the husband was dead and this old lady was a little senile. Just as that thought raced across his mind he turned around and came face to face with the old man. It startled Dave to the point where he fell back to the ground in shock. He quickly composed himself and escorted the man to the upper balcony where he and his wife would be hoisted to safety.

When asked what he thought about everything that was going on in New Orleans, Dave told us that he could not believe this was America. It just looked like a third world country, the whole situation was very depressing. Dave was forced to compartmentalize what he was feeling and press on to get the job done. This is a powerful statement and very true. New Orleans was devastated and it just didn't look anything like the city we all knew and loved. A key point to remember is that a large majority of the people being rescued were some of the poorest in the nation, who didn't have the means to get out. The Coast Guard was able to rescue a lot of people, but many of the weak and sick that didn't get picked up the first couple of days just didn't make it. The sight of dead bodies floating down the street was typical, but not something these Coast Guard heroes focused on.

On one particular rescue Dave picked up a guy whose dead brother was slumped over in a wheel chair in the balcony below. The guy asked for his brother's body to be hoisted up too, but Dave explained that saving lives was the priority and that the Coast Guard doesn't typically transport dead bodies. It sounds tough, but that's really what had to be said. "We had to focus on the ones that were still alive. There were still a lot of people to be saved, so none of us focused on the tragedies. We stayed positive and focused on the next life we could impact in a positive manner."

Dave McClure is a true hero and a testament to what hard work and dedication can do to a man. From his humble beginnings and wrong turns in life, Dave pushed on and has become part of a truly elite team. At 23 years of age, he probably doesn't realize the extent of his contribution to this great nation. Operating in a dangerous and new environment, Dave stepped up to the plate like an old pro. He was able to conquer all his doubts and fears and do what he was meant to do. As the motto goes, he risked it all "So Others May Live." Dave will forever be linked to every single person he saved and to the Hurricane Katrina Rescue Efforts. His rescues are sure to be the topic of conversation at Thanksgiving dinners for many years to come.

AST3 David McClure was awarded the Distinguished Flying Cross for his services to his country during post Hurricane Katrina operations. It is one of the highest awards that the President of the United States may bestow on a service member. There are 224 people still here on earth with us thanks to this young, brave man's actions.

CHAPTER SEVEN

AIRCRAFT COMMANDER
Lt. Jason Smith

7

There are three ways to become a Coast Guard Officer, one can attend the Coast Guard Academy, be commissioned through the Officer Candidate School or enter the service as a Direct Commissioned Officer from one of the other four branches of the Armed Forces. Jason Scott Smith is one of those Direct Commissioned Officers. He started as an Officer in the Army before "lateraling-over" to the Coast Guard. It is not an easy decision for those guys and gals that commit to making the jump. One of the primary factors these officers must consider is money and not just getting a raise either, some of these officers actually get demoted and take a pay-cut to come into the Coast Guard. In most cases it is a drop from the rank of LT or CPT (0-3) to LTJG (0-2). That is a significant loss of pay and status, one that can effect the decision to change from one branch of service to another. In Jason Smith's case he considered losing the extra pay worth-while after the things he had seen and experienced as an Army Apache Pilot. His family needed a change and the Coast Guard was his way of providing that.

A true Texas boy, brimming with spirit and confidence, Jason is originally from Houston. He was born there on December 27, 1971 but moved with his family as an infant to Medicine Hat Alberta Canada, where they lived until he was six years old. His father Chester had an opportunity to establish his career as a Chiropractor in the socialized medical system in Canada. With an opportunity such as this, the Smiths had no choice and packed up their things and headed north. It was a significant change for his mother Terri and her family. Terri's mother had to watch her daughter and grandchildren venture away to another country some twenty-five hundred miles almost due north from their home in Texas. Although there was some struggle, the opportunity was too great and the rest of the family ultimately supported the decision.

After establishing his profession and practicing in the specialty for several years, it was time for Chester and the gang to return to Houston. This time his career led them back to Houston where he was offered a position as a professor at the Chiropractic College of Houston. They spent a couple of years in Houston and then moved once more, this time to the small town of Lexington, TX. A rural town of 1,500 or so, Lexington is where Jason spent the rest of his years up until he joined the Army. Something occurred to Jason after they moved back to Texas. During junior high school Jason learned about the Vietnam War and he had an eerie notion for a time that maybe his father had fled to Canada to avoid the draft. He knows now that was not the case, but he still jokes about the whole family piling into a yellow Volkswagen bus with big flowers painted on its sides so the family could flee north escaping his dad's draft number in Canada, totally not true, but humorous for Jason to use as a story sometimes.

In addition to learning about the Vietnam War, Junior High School was also when Jason made his decision to join the military. With his grandfather serving in World War II and his Uncle serving in Vietnam, one could say that military service was what he was born to do. What sealed the deal for Jason was a conversation he had with his Uncle regarding life in the military and the Vietnam War. Junior High School seems to be a rather early age for a young man to make that sort of commitment, but that is the type of guy that Jason is. He started writing letters to his local congressman in hopes of gaining an appointment to the Air Force Academy. This went on until he was in high school. When the time came, Jason went to the county seat to meet with his representative, but the meeting did not go the way Jason had envisioned it would. After all his letter writing and planning, Jason didn't even get to meet with the man he hoped would bless him with the appointment, he met with an aide. The aide informed Jason that the Air Force slot had already been given to another candidate, so he wouldn't be able to attend.

The aide told Jason that there was hope for an appointment to West Point or maybe the Naval Academy, but Jason did not know much about those schools and he still had his heart set on the Air Force. The politics of the whole situation left him a little deflated but not without hope. Jason decided to attend Sam Houston State College in Huntsville, Texas not far from his home in Lexington. During his first couple of years, he bounced around from major to major not really deciding on an area of concentration. That pattern of jumping around majors changed his third year of college when he joined the Army Reserve Officers' Training Corp (ROTC). He had been playing lacrosse for a while when his ROTC buddies offered him a spot on a team they had put together for the Army's Ranger Challenge competition. Ranger Challenge is a three-day decathlon type competition between ROTC squads from around the region. Their team did well enough to earn a spot at the national finals held at Fort Lewis in Washington State, with Jason's skill being a key catalyst to their success.

After the finals each year the Brigade Commander has the option of granting one incentive scholarship to an outstanding cadet. Jason's performance so impressed the Commander that he selected Jason for the scholarship. That was the push he needed. Jason accepted the scholarship and used it to finish two more years of school and completed his bachelor's degree. Although it took a total of five and a half years of college for him to get his degree, Jason figures that was way ahead of schedule for him. Upon graduation Jason was commissioned as a Second Lieutenant in the United States Army and selected for the Army's Flight Training Program.

Jason's commissioning as an Army Officer took place in 1995, concurrent with another significant event in his life. In 1995 Jason also married his childhood sweetheart, Julie, who he had known since the 5th grade and dated in High School. Julie had recently completed nursing school and was ready to start a new life with her recently roped husband. They started off the adventure by leaving Texas and moving to Fort Rucker in Alabama. All Army would-be Pilots start their flying careers at Fort Rucker, where they spend months learning two things, the fundamentals of Army Officer Leadership and how to fly helicopters.

After graduation, Jason was selected to transition to the Apache attack helicopter. The transition went smoothly and afterwards he accepted orders to Germany, his first Army duty station. Their first six months in Germany Julie and Jason enjoyed the country and were afforded the opportunity to travel. They had some good times until the Bosnian Conflict started. During this conflict in Bosnia, Jason was deployed as a Platoon Leader in support of this peacekeeping mission. Jason remembers it as a very confusing time with all the different factions that were a part of the skirmish. He also remembers the deployment as a great learning experience for him as a junior Aviator and Platoon Leader. The mountainous terrain and high altitudes taught him how to fly the Apache at its full limits. Needless to say, his first deployment separated him from his wife but taught him many lessons he would keep with him throughout the rest of his career as a Military Officer.

After Bosnia, Jason returned to Germany. Things slowed down somewhat and were relatively normal, until war broke out in Kosovo. During that war, Jason served as a Corps Aviation Planner, where he prepared Apaches for deployment and supported the helicopter's missions. When his rotation time came, the Army cut orders for Jason and his family to Fort Campbell in Kentucky. In conjunction with the move he would have to attend 9 months of additional training at Fort Rucker, only it wasn't just Jason and Julie this time. They had their daughter Reagan with them this time, who was born while they were stationed in Germany. A stressful yet exciting part of military life is the aspect of moving every few years. Sometimes it can take a toll on the family, but nevertheless, starting a fresh adventure with a new baby keeps a family on their toes.

At Fort Campbell, Jason served the Army in a position of much higher responsibility. This time, the Army made him a Company Commander, in charge of eight Apache Helicopters with sixteen Pilots and support personnel. He managed the day-to-day operations of the company and its readiness. Regular readiness training and preparations went on until that fateful day in September referred to as "9-11". Jason remembers first hearing about the attack while he was working-out in the gym. He said, "When I heard the commentator say a plane had flown into the World Trade center, my first thought was that maybe a Cessna had some sort of problem and accidentally collided with one of the buildings. But when I heard of the second plane crashing into the other building I knew something was wrong. My phone immediately started ringing and would not stop. It was my crew. The wanted to know what was going on. They wanted to know what our orders were."

Jason did not consider himself just a Company Commander, he was a member of the 101st, a ready division on standby for worldwide deployment within thirty-six hours. He took pride in that, and it was his duty to have his company "palletized" for shipment right away. Anticipating the order and ensuring that his troops were ready to answer the call, Jason gave the orders to have all pre-deployment checks complete. Good thing too, just as his men reported that they were complete, the order came down from his superiors for his company to mobilize. The 101st "stood-up" and was on the airfield ready to go the evening of September 11, 2001. They didn't go anywhere however because the destination of the mission was not yet determined. The division "stood down" to lay-in-wait for the next order. It came shortly after, the 101st was ordered to rendezvous in Afghanistan for immediate combat.

C-17 cargo aircraft from the Air Force were the means of transportation for the troops and their equipment from Fort Campbell to Kandahar, Afghanistan. Each of the advanced cargo planes could carry two Apaches, its crews and enough support equipment to be a self-sustaining unit. Jason remembers seeing C-17s lined up along the tarmac waiting to be loaded with their cargo. One after the other, they rotated through Fort Campbell for days, loading and departing. Jason's company was one of the first to leave.

"I remember stepping off the C-17 and the heat just hitting me like a blowtorch. It was a completely different environment, just hours before we had been in the comfortable surroundings of Fort Campbell and its nice climate, but Afghanistan was a completely different world. The first few minutes were quite surreal, but then reality set-in and I realized I had to get to work." The maintenance crews had the Apaches off loaded and put back together in about four hours. The only information that the Pilots were given was that they had to takeoff and head for Bagram. The alpha model Apaches were loaded to the max with fuel and weapons for the transit. There was no guidance from superiors except to get there, so they all took off. Enroute, the flight of two helicopters flew over weapons sites and troops, not knowing if they were combatants or friendly. Regardless, the birds of prey stayed low and made the run without incident.

Once in Bagram the crews found out they were the tip of the arrow for Operation Anaconda. "The fight" was an hour's flight to the north. Jason quickly calculated what that meant as far as time on-scene and realized that his Apaches could get there, fight for about forty five minutes, and then return to home base. There was one big obstacle between them and the fight though, it was a mountain range that had to be crossed at a pass about eleven thousand feet. This is not a supremely difficult task in a normal situation, but this was not normal, there were people that wanted the

American choppers to fall out of the sky in big balls of flames, and they would do their very best to make that happen. Jason was always uncomfortable making the climb through the pass and his concerns literally blew up in his face one day.

Jason told of an event that changed his life forever with a matter of fact look in his eyes. It was a sobering look that would leave a packed convention hall silent. This event occurred on his third or fourth time crossing the mountains. There was a road that wound up the ridge. It was a road that all the Pilots knew, was a potential ambush area. He was flying lead in a flight of two Apaches, both helicopters loaded. The weapons systems were slaved to the pilot's helmets, so whatever they looked at was in their sights and could be shot down. "We were tense every time we crossed, but this time as we were reaching the top of the climb I saw a white van. It looked like the typical terrorist type van from the news clips. Just as we were at our slowest point and only a few seconds from reaching the peak, I saw the van come to an abrupt stop. At this point we were basically sitting ducks, and wouldn't you know it, out pops a person with a long black tube. Sure enough, he threw the tube onto his shoulder, my back tensed up and I knew the next thing was the impact."

His wingman, Todd was there and on his trigger, the only thing Jason could get out over the radio was, "SAM! SAM! SAM!" Lucky for Jason, Todd turned and looked right at the van and pulled the trigger. Instead of getting shot down by whatever it was, there was an explosion and the side of mountain that erupted in dirt and debris. "To this day I know he saved my life, my butt was gone without his shot. I wouldn't be here for you, my kids or anyone if Todd would have hesitated." It was sobering listening to the story and knowing that war is permanent for the troops, one way or the other its memory never goes away. After the explosion they nosed-over, never looking back and continued on into the valley floor to join the fight.

Jason remained in the fight in Afghanistan until September of 2002. By that time he had made the decision to join the Coast Guard. He had told his Brigade Commander of his decision to transfer to the sea going service, so it was no secret. His command and his men knew that he would eventually be leaving them. His decision weighed on Jason a little bit. After all, everyone knew that Iraq was going to be the next fight, it was simply inevitable. When the order came to deploy and remove Saddam

Hussein, Jason agreed to lead his men into battle one more time for the Iraqi deployment. That would be his last chance to fight with them. He knew they could handle the job without him, but they were his family and he just didn't feel right leaving them when there was a job to get done.

Once again, Jason and his troops were a part of the first wave of the attack. This time they went to Kuwait for staging. Jason was a senior Aviator at this point and had been seasoned with years of combat experience. Having experience allows a Pilot to train the new guys, but it doesn't make them bullet proof, as Jason would discover on another mission. His group was tasked with a diversion mission in support of the main attack. Jason's company was ordered into Iraq as part of a "Faint", which is an attack wave meant to fool the enemy and occupy the opposing forces while the main element assaults in a different area.

"When a faint works well the bad guys really believe they are being attacked", Jason explained. "Our first mission was to recon areas for prep-fire that was artillery fire meant to clear out any civilians and flush out bad guys. It always amazed me that the native people would go about their lives hanging out cloths, herding goats or whatever they would normally do in the midst of a war, but they do. Anyway, we had to check out sites to minimize the civilian casualties, and no matter how the media portrays us, we really try to keep from hurting noncombatants. Eventually we found a few sites with activity and did our job. The following mission was to support the tanks rolling in. They had to follow roads because of canals that ran the land. We would lead the tanks by a few miles to see if there were any bad guys waiting for them. Well we found some that day."

Assigned a young co-pilot, Jason was going to use the patrol time to do a little training. He thought that he could teach the rookie a few things about combat maneuvering, so he took the controls and demonstrated evasive flying techniques to keep from being a stable target. Out of the corner of his eye he saw some movement on the ground. He banked his Apache hard to the right and kicked the tail around to come on the target in an attack position. As the helicopter came around, Jason could feel the airframe taking rounds, then he felt a sharp pain in his face and numbness flowed across his right jaw and cheek. He instinctively stabled out the aircraft and passed the controls to his young co-pilot in the back, something that proved to be a life saver for his young co-pilot later.

The situation was not good, Jason, the senior Pilot, was in the front of the helicopter and at that point thinks he just lost half of his face, while the junior pilot in the back can not see to confirm whether Jason has a jaw left or not as the enemy is set to attack the tanks. What seemed like minutes, but was actually only a few seconds went by and Jason realized he could still feel his teeth and could also still talk. "My first thought was that I would be going through the rest of my life without my jaw or at least part of the right side of my face, but when I realized all the bones were still there I refocused on my tankers on the ground. One of my silly concerns was letting my guys know what happened to me without sounding like a wimp on the radio." It's amazing the things that go through someone's mind even during time of war.

"I called the 05 commander in charge of the battle and told him we had been hit and that he needed to lay fire on the location of the source. The tank guys take care of us as much as we take care of them, so they moved in fast to clear out the threat. I called my sister ship to lead us to the medics and we flew to that location. My co-pilot did a great job of getting us there and executing a textbook approach in the brownout conditions at the landing zone (LZ). When they evaluated me they said I would live but wanted me to stay for a few days. I wouldn't have any of that, I told them to put a band-aid on it and send me the bill, I had tanks to cover. We saddled up and went back to the fight."

After assessing the damage to the aircraft and recovering some slugs, Jason discovered that the most probable explanation of the events was that his helicopter started taking fire, and an AK-47 round came through the lower area of the helicopter to the right of his seat. The round of ammunition tumbled until it struck him in the cheek and nose and then hit his night vision goggle mount blowing it off his helmet. When he rolled the helicopter level it may have saved the co-pilot in the back seat, because there was a continuous trail of holes from ammunition rounds running from the front to the back of the cockpit area. The trail of rounds would have been at the co-pilot's head if the helicopter had not been rolled level. After they were airborne enroute back to the fight, the weapons arming system failed because of a wire bundle that had been damaged by a round in the pylon. As crazy as it sounds, they went back to war without the ability to defend themselves. Jason figures it was all in a days work.

The battle they started lasted through the next day and moved all the way to the Baghdad city limits before the faint was cancelled and the main force moved on the city from a different direction. Almost every helicopter took hits during the battle, but the company did not loose a single aircraft in the course of the attack. In fact, only one was damaged beyond repair. At the rally point, one of the helicopters actually had the unexploded tip of an RPG stuck in its tail boom that would have definitely knocked the bird out of the sky if it had worked properly. Thank God for inferior foreign weapon design and construction. If that were an American made grenade, it would have worked.

Jason explained that he was never happier or more satisfied with his job in the Army than when he was in the field. He had no problems fighting, training or performing any aspect of his job, but he had a commitment to his family and going to war was keeping him from his obligation of taking care of them.

He added it up. His time with his two-year-old son Zane and the outcome was not surprising. Out of his new son's first two years of life, Jason had spent no more than 5 months with Zane. His daughter Reagan had lived a similar fate. Post 9/11 he also had the personal feeling that taking care of the fight back home was important. After all, the most recent fight was brought to America. We didn't ask the leaders of radical Islam to fly jets into the World Trade Center Buildings. If those demented people, who interpret a religion as a death sentence for all nonbelievers, will kill themselves to kill innocent Americans, then what is going to happen next and who was going to stop them inside our borders? So Jason was ready to defend the sovereign shores of the United States joining the Department of Homeland Security by becoming a Pilot in the U.S. Coast Guard.

August 2003 Jason was sworn-in as a Lieutenant Junior Grade in the United States Coast Guard. He was treated very well by the recruiters and was pleasantly impressed that they took the time to help his family so much. During the process he had been stuck in the Army fighting a war and could not handle many of the paperwork issues that need to be cleared up. "The recruiter actually called Julie and kept her informed of what was going on with the transition. I thought that this organization must really care about its people if this is how things work. I was not wrong. The detailer went out of his way to keep a spot open for me until I was released

from the Army. I was extremely surprised at how much care was taken in my personal case."

Jason was given orders to Air Station Houston, right where he wanted and deserved to go. He and Julie established a home and started living life a little more normal, at least in comparison to the life they had lead in the Army. Nine months after arriving in Houston they had their third child, Walker. They must have been pretty happy to be in Houston, happy enough to make a transfer baby. When Jason arrived at the Air Station he was just like any other new Direct Commissioned Aviator (DCA), except he had sharper talents and a whole lot more medals to wear on his uniform. The other Pilots stationed at Air Station Houston knew he was a war hero, the medals gave him away.

Even heroes have to learn new tricks though, and Jason was no exception
to the rule. Hovering low over the water at night was a talent that Jason
admits took him a great deal of practice to master. Coast Guard flying is
quite different from every other type of flying, mainly because when the
weather gets crappy everyone else in the world puts their aircrafts to bed
and calls it a day. Wars are even stopped because of bad weather, but the
Coast Guard Aviators crank up and go in the worst type of conditions.
They are literally the most highly skilled and bravest "bad weather" Pilots
in the world. Even the President of the United States has commented on
how the Coast Guard is able to fly in weather that other military Aviators
refuse to take part in.

Jason progressed rapidly through the training to become a First Pilot and he did the same with the Aircraft Commander syllabus. He became a Senior Duty Officer and worked in the Administration Department until a little lady name Katrina came calling. Jason remembers hanging out with some guys from Air Station New Orleans that had evacuated to Houston. It wasn't the first time they had evacuated and everyone knew it wouldn't be the last. With the approach of a category five hurricane, people were anxious, excited and ready to go rescue whoever needed it after the storm had passed.

Because of the way the duty schedule worked out, Jason was one of two Aircraft Commanders available to leave for New Orleans. His leaving would have the least amount of impact on the rest of the crew and the already burdened duty rotation. The Operations Officer told him that right after the weather was within limits to launch, he was to take a helicopter and crew in behind Katrina accompanying the crews from New Orleans back to affect rescue. Jason was ready, willing and able to go and of course somewhat anxious. To have the opportunity to take a ten million dollar helicopter and a highly trained crew to rescue people after a hurricane, well that was an honor and an adrenaline rush all in one. He prepared for the trip on the evening of August 28th, packing his bag and a few snacks in case food was scarce.

Jason and his crew launched mid morning on August 29th following behind the Air Station New Orleans' helicopters. Jason's first mission was to pick up a CWO navigation expert from the CG to help assess the impact of the hurricane on the Maritime Navigational Aids such as buoys and markers. They landed at a remote airfield west of New Orleans to pick up this expert and to gas up before heading into the devastation. Just as they were landing they saw the Air Station New Orleans helicopters take off. They met up with the navigation expert and briefed him up on the situation. They made it clear that SAR was a priority and that if need be, they would drop him off to make room for survivors. The CWO agreed and hopped in the helicopter and off to New Orleans they went.

West of the city the radios started coming alive with traffic. There were calls coming from everyone with a radio. "It was utter chaos. We landed at Air Station New Orleans and dropped off the navigation guy we had picked up. We also unloaded our bags because we needed the cabin space for survivors. We then immediately launched again to start searching. We headed south to help the other crews that were already in the middle of rescues." Since the area south of the city was covered by crews from Air Station New Orleans and the other Houston crew, Jason decided to head east. A few miles away from the city on the east side he started to hear chatter on the radio. The radio traffic indicated that helicopter crews from the Coast Guard Aviation Training Center (ATC Mobile) were already east of the city performing rescues. ATC is located in Mobile, AL with its primary mission being to train Coast Guard Pilots. Although they typically do not conduct Search and Rescue, the large number of helicopters and crews at Mobile were desperately needed for a large-scale operation such as the relief efforts following Hurricane Katrina. Realizing that ATC could handle anything from Alabama to Mississippi and into eastern Louisiana, Jason decided to take his crew north and assess the situation. As they passed over the city, reality set in and for the first time Jason realized the tremendous amount of people that stayed behind and would eventually need assistance.

As far as he knows, Jason and his crew were the first to recon the northern part of the city. The canal levees had already broken and flooded the north side of town, leaving only rooftops as the visible parts of the homes in the area. For a Coast Guard Pilot, the easy part is plucking someone from the clutches of death. The hard part for Jason was what to do with the survivors after they were rescued. Some of the questions going through his mind were "where do we take these people, will they be safe and can they be reached by a larger transport vehicle?" This was one of the biggest difficulties faced by rescue aircrews the first few days. No one really knew where they were supposed to drop off survivors. Jason's crew actually took people to the Super Dome the first day, as it was communicated over the radios that the Super Dome was accepting people and would be transporting them over to Houston, TX.

The wind was still gusting between 50 to 70 Knots. The weather was very challenging early after the storm had moved north, but the crew managed the high winds and intermittent rain. Jason's helicopter had arrived about six hours after Katrina made landfall. With New Orleans being inland and the storm measuring hundreds of miles across, that essentially put all of those crews on the backside of the storm. Dealing with gusting winds is difficult in a helicopter, especially when hovering. Wind is just like airspeed to a helicopter, in a hover, if the wind changes from 50 to 70 knots in a split second, control inputs must be made rapidly to keep the helicopter from moving. With a rescue swimmer dangling between power lines, trees and apartment walls, the helicopter needs to stay in place. With the wind changes as erratic as they were, Jason had to remain ever vigilant and reactive to the changes that were taking place.

The Belle Chasse Football Field eventually became the drop off point of choice for Jason and his crew. It was conveniently located to where they were performing their rescues, and buses were setup to transport the survivors. Additionally, ambulance and minimal medical care was available. It was a bit difficult to get the helicopters in and out, but the area was large enough to land and it could accommodate many survivors. One of the early concerns for Jason was families getting separated. With everything else an Aircraft Commander has to think about in that type of demanding situation, having the composure to pay attention to that sort of detail is a testament to Jason's maturity as an on-scene commander and seasoned leader in the helicopter. Trying to keep families together is extremely difficult with the variables that exist. First, the helicopter can hold only a few people at one time. Second, if the helicopter needs fuel then it has to leave no matter what. Third, if in the middle of picking-up part of a family there is a more perilous situation, the crew must depart because the more desperate case becomes the priority. Jason had to manage all these types of scenarios, but thankfully he never had to separate children from their parents.

Jason flew on many cases, but there are a few standouts because the circumstances and challenges are so far off the scale that they stuck with him. One such case for Jason happened on his first night in the New Orleans area. He had come into a hover over a "John Boat" tied to a tree. His crew got rigged and ready and then hoisted down the Rescue Swimmer to assess the situation and report his recommendations back to the helicopter. Once down on-scene, the swimmer observed that the people in the boat was not the most critical issue, but rather the grandmother of those people who was floating a few feet away on a mattress with life sustaining equipment. Those types of variables can complicate a rescue real fast.

Adding to the critical nature of the situation was the fact that his helicopter was only minutes away from running out of fuel. Jason communicated this over the radio to his Rescue Swimmer only to be informed that getting the lady ready for pick-up would take much more time than the few minutes Jason couldn't afford to remain on scene. Reluctantly, Jason was forced to make the tough decision to leave his Rescue Swimmer on scene to prepare the lady while he took the helicopter for fuel. To make matters worse, Jason and his crew were already on one flight time extension (crews can only fly 6 hours at a time) and coming back for the survivor and the Swimmer would require a second extension. Following procedure, Jason marked the Swimmer's position and headed back for fuel and to discuss a flight time extension with the Operational Commander.

Upon arrival at Air Station New Orleans, Jason went in to talk with his OPS boss and informed him that he knew exactly where the swimmer was and that he wanted to go back for him and the survivors. The OPS boss asked Jason how the crew was holding up. Jason assured him that everyone was still on top of their game. The Commander granted the crew another extension to recover the swimmer, complete the case and return to base to let fresh pilots take over the mission. Like a good Coastie, Jason's reply was "Roger-that sir," as he rushed back to his helicopter to get back on scene.

When the helicopter arrived on scene, the Rescue Swimmer had decided to recover the elderly incapacitated woman utilizing the Double-Lift Method. This meant that he would come up with her holding the medical equipment she had attached to her. The hoisting evolution was going to be tight, so to make it happen, Jason had to hover the helicopter between some gigantic trees, thread the cable down to the swimmer and than reverse that entire scenario to retrieve the woman. It was close and the cable became fouled on the way down, but the Flight Mechanic did an excellent job providing conning commands to keep the helicopter in position and was able to control to hoist cable effectively to complete the rescue safely. The key to any successful hoist or rescue that requires precise aircraft positioning is the coordination between the Pilot and the Flight Mechanic. It is imperative in a case such as this one that the Flight Mechanic's conning commands be short and explicit and that the Pilot have the trust and confidence to follow the commands. The crew coordination in this case was top notch and the maneuver ended up going a lot smoother than Jason had anticipated.
Once the woman was aboard, the crew had another dilemma. Where would they take her? After all, she's not like any of the cases they had

dealt with previously, this lady needed real emergency medical care. She could not simply be taken to dry ground, she desperately needed medical attention. The problem was, all the hospitals were impacted by Katrina as well and didn't have electricity, staff or even the space to take in another patient. Jason wasn't even sure if any medical staff was manning the hospitals.

Jason and his crew eventually found a hospital, and although all the lights were off, they decided to land anyway. Once they were on top of the building, the normal scenario would be that ER nurses would come to the helicopter with a gurney, unload the patient and whisk her away to get medical care. That wouldn't be the case this time. No one came out, no one called on the radio, and no one turned the lights on. After a minute or so, Jason sent his Flight Mechanic Brian in to see what was going on. Brian came back a few minutes later and informed the rest of the crew that the power was off in the hospital, which meant there was no elevator service to the roof. This meant that would need to carry the woman down a number of floors for her to get emergency care.

The Flight Mechanic and Swimmer left the rooftop with the woman and took her to safety in the hospital. They were gone for quite a while, long enough to make Jason concerned because they were running out of time and fuel and another extension would have gotten Jason in some real trouble with the OPS boss. Just before he started calling the Swimmer on the radio or worse yet have to send his co-pilot out to look for them, the guys emerged from the blackened hospital door and onto the roof. After such a long days work and all the rescues they completed, the crew headed back for a well deserved rest. Little did they know there were no beds to sleep in, no air condition (power was out) and no water for a shower.

Tuesday came and operations in the area picked up greatly. The weather had cleared up and more helicopters were working the area to try and help, especially helicopters from other services that wouldn't come fly when it was real nasty out. Lots of helicopters in the sky are good for the victims, but this increases the risk of mid-air collisions. Pilots now had to be extremely cautious of their surroundings and practice "defensive flying". Making that ever present danger even worse was that there was no established communications plan. Some of the different agencies didn't even have the same types of radios as the others. Talking to other crews was a real problem.

Jason had been hearing some chatter on the radios regarding a need for specific medications. It seemed that there were a lot of requests for insulin. Hearing that the city had been tapped out for medicine, Jason and his crew headed north to the town of Slidell to assess the damage in that area with hopes that they could find a hospital with insulin to spare. They found the Slidell area to be better off than New Orleans.

Much to their surprise, the Slidell hospital was open and had power. Jason landed and had his crew see if the hospital had any extra insulin. It turns out they had a lot of it, so Jason made the decision to take all this insulin back to New Orleans and get it to the people that needed it. The crew was able to make contact with an ambulance that was willing to act as a distribution point for the medication. They dropped off their supplies and let the professionals take care of the diabetes patients that were in need.

Fast rational thinking is what Coast Guard Pilots are known for. That is what makes them so effective in situations of desperation, when there is no other form of structured control. Other agencies do not give their Pilots the autonomy to act independent of direct orders. There were cases where training helicopters from Pensacola stopped to help Katrina victims, and those pilots were reprimanded for not flying straight back to their home station. Never will a Coast Guard Pilot be questioned about using reasonable judgment to save a life. That's what separates a Coast Guard Pilot from all others. Saving lives comes first, always. We all understand that!

As time went on the desperation of the people affected worsened. Then the worse occurred. The levee along Lake Pontchartrain broke and the lake began draining into the city making an already terrible situation even more horrific. Operations picked up fast. Rescue calls were coming in faster than the crews could manage to get to them. A sense of urgency filled Air Station New Orleans as everyone realized that the dry parts of the city were about to become flooded and that more people were going to be in harms way.

On August 30th the main drop off point became Lake Front Airport. It was located just northeast of the city and the water had receded enough from the previous day to use it as a rally point. It's location to the newly flooded areas made Lake Front Airport a great spot to drop off survivors, however, there was limited access to Lake Front Airport because there was flooding in the areas immediately surrounding it. After a while the situation became tense. People were getting dropped off, but there was nowhere for them to go and no transportation to take them. Rival gangs were starting to cause problems and attempting to take over these drop-off points. Not knowing what to do, Jason had his Flight Mechanic and Rescue Swimmer tell the local officials at the airport to have the crowd clear the runway of debris so that a C-130 could land and transport them to safety. Granted this was just a hunch, and although Jason had seen a C-130 flying low over the runway earlier that day, there was no guarantee that it was coming back the same day. This course of action did however get all the survivors working as a team towards a common goal and kept everyone pre-occupied with clearing the runway rather than causing trouble.

As restless as everyone was getting, the crews started to worry about their personal safety at various drop-off locations. The University of New Orleans was one of the drop-off points were Jason had taken several loads of people. Each time they landed the mob grew angrier and angrier about the conditions they were suffering through. Although they were dry and safe, those folks were not happy. It got so bad, that Jason had to keep power on the helicopter in order to blow the mob back when he landed. The Rescue Swimmer and Flight Mechanic had to take an aggressive posture to keep the people from moving towards the helicopter. Times were becoming uncomfortable for Jason and his crew, even though they were the good guys. It was definitely a scary experience.

Meanwhile, his plan at Lake Front Airport worked and the next time they landed the runways had been cleared of all debris. The C-130 did not come back on the 30th due to other tasking it had received, but when it finally did the runway was clear and the C-130 could land safely and evacuate a huge percentage of the survivors. Unlike the helicopters, the C-130s can carry many more people and fly a longer distance to safety. That is why it was so important to clear that runway.

When asked, what his most memorable moment was Jason had to think just for a second, then he replied, "It wasn't a rescue, it was an event. You see there was this old man, I can't remember if we had rescued him and dropped him off at Lake Front, but every time we landed he would be looking at the helicopter and would try to approach it. If you told me he was ninety I would believe it. One of the last times we landed there he tried to approach the helicopter again, this time I wanted to know what he wanted, so I asked one of my crew members to go see what this old man wanted from us. Well come to find out, he was picked up and for some reason his wife was left behind for another trip. He was looking for his wife to get off the helicopter every time one of them landed. He wanted to know if we could go back to his house and check on his bride."

You know how hard it is to find anything in a flooded and damaged city? Even with an address and description it is worse than finding a needle in a haystack. It's more like finding a needle in a hayfield. "If there were anything I could have done to help him I would have, but there just wasn't anyway of getting there and trying would pull us away from attainable rescues of people that we knew we could help. That brought it all home for me. I don't know for sure, but they could have been married for sixty or seventy years and he just wanted to know if she was alright. If there was one thing I could've done that I didn't get to do while I was there was to reunite him with his bride."

Although you can't save them all, Jason's efforts and those of Coast Guard helicopter crews everywhere were instrumental in the success of Hurricane Katrina Rescue Operations. Jason was personally responsible for saving over 170 lives and spent close to a week's time in New Orleans. The days were long and day-to-day comforts were not present. They often times went without much to eat, a comfortable place to sleep or even a shower. These luxuries we take for granted, heroes like Jason did without in order to save others. Times like these require dedicated men and women who will sacrifice their time for the greater good of the nation. Just as he did with selfless service in the Army, Jason continues to do his nation proud saving lives as a Coast Guard Rescue Pilot. Jason earned a United States Air Medal for his heroic service in support of Hurricane Katrina relief efforts.

CHAPTER EIGHT

A JOB WELL DONE
Semper Paratus

8

Our humble Coasties truly answered
the call of the nation. They impacted
survivors they will never see again and
saved lives of those who may never get
a chance to say thanks. In the course
of action, while responding to Katrina, the Coast Guard saved or moved
33,500 people in the week after Katrina made landfall. These unsung
heroes gave it their all expecting nothing in return. They are content with
the satisfaction that their occupation provides them. The Coast Guard
stood out as the first responders, capable of fast decisive action to tragedy,
unhampered by the politics of the day. For the men and women that left
their families to help those in need, it was refreshing to get the national
focus that the Coast Guard deserves.

No other organization is capable of the immediate mobilization that the
Coast Guard has developed over the years. Because of its charter, whose
basic principles were founded with the Revenue Cutter Service in 1790,
the Coast Guard has evolved into the premier service for Homeland Security. Inevitable disasters, day-to-day security and rescuing those in peril
requires a national force that is agile and strong. Katrina was a coming
of age for the Coast Guard, there is no turning back. Since becoming a
member of the Department of Homeland Security the Coast Guard has
shouldered more responsibility than most are aware of. It is the only multi
mission service standing watch over our country with the diverse assets
and leadership to manage large scale disasters.

When a significant event takes place like Katrina or 9-11 the local responders are either affected personally or overwhelmed in the immediate hours post event. The Coast Guard is dispersed about the country in
small towns and large cities with a national structure and communication
chain that empowers every level of the organization to make a decision.

The leaders answer to the Secretary of Homeland Security, after responding, there is no hesitation and that is what makes them so valuable to the country.

The Coast Guard is now involved with every aspect of Homeland Security. It is responsible for the cargo coming into the country via ship, it patrols our country's borders and investigates potential terrorist threats. Coasties provide security for the countries largest oil refineries and are airborne, helping to keep the President safe when he travels domestically. Coast Guard ships patrol the Bering Sea enforcing fisheries laws to ensure our national marine resources are not poached or over-burdened. Once the youngest and newest are sworn into the Coast Guard they are expected to be a multi-faceted servant of our country, to embrace a proud tradition of national pride dating back to the colonial days.

Katrina was the stage for the Coast Guard to show how capable it really is. The individual Coasties are the back bone of the service and make it strong. These honorable and selfless individuals are incredibly devoted to serving their country. Given the opportunity, they will risk it all "So others may live". That is something built into there character, not something taught to them. The Coast Guard attracts that type of person. Thank God for that!!

Below is a list of the medals awarded to the heroes in this book.

The Distinguished Flying Cross
AST3 David McClure

The Air Medal
LT Sean O'Brien   LT Jason Smith
LT Charles Guerrero   AST3 Charles Medema

These medals are great honors to receive and only awarded to service members who standout for their particular actions. The following is a description of the two medals, The Distinguished Flying Cross is the higher of the two.

"The Distinguished Flying Cross may be awarded to military members who, while serving in any capacity with the Armed Forces, distinguish themselves by heroism or outstanding achievement while participating in aerial flight. To be awarded for heroism the act must involve voluntary action in the face of danger and be well above the actions performed by others engaged in similar flight operations. If awarded for extraordinary achievement, it must have resulted in an accomplishment so exceptional and outstanding as to clearly set the individual apart from his or her comrades or from other persons in similar circumstances."
—Direct quote taken from Awards Manual

"The Air Medal may be awarded to individuals who, while serving in any capacity with the Armed Forces, distinguish themselves by heroism, outstanding achievement, or by meritorious service while participating in aerial flight."
—Direct quote taken from Awards Manual

In the end, the sacrifice and commitment made by Coast Guard men and women nationwide saved thousands of lives, and although this book only featured 5 of the more extraordinary Coasties, the service as a whole came together once again to the aid of our great nation. If you are a Coastie reading this, thank you for your service. If you are not, thanks for your interest and support of this great organization.

The Coast Guard remained on-scene in the area even after the initial rescues were complete. On September 9, 2005, Secretary Chertoff appointed VADM Thad Allen as the Principal Federal Official responsible for the entire federal response and recovery effort. This ensured the Coast Guard's continued presence in the area and was a great compliment to the service. For the first time in years, the Coast Guard was getting the credit it deserved and VADM Allen's appointment signified that top government officials realized the Coast Guard was the right organization to lead this effort.

To purchase a signed copy of this book or to order bulk quantities at a discount visit www.therealguardians.com.